"History will judge us by the difference we make in the everyday lives of children."
—Nelson Mandela

Sweet Carolina MYSTERIES

Roots and Wings
Picture-Perfect Mystery
Angels Watching Over Me
A Change of Art
Conscious Decisions
Surrounded by Mercy
Broken Bonds
Mercy's Healing
To Heal a Heart
A Cross to Bear
Merciful Secrecy

Sweet Carolina MYSTERIES

MERCIFUL SECRECY

Ruth Logan Herne

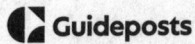

Sweet Carolina Mysteries is a trademark of Guideposts.

Published by Guideposts Books & Inspirational Media
100 Reserve Road, Suite E200
Danbury, CT 06810
Guideposts.org

Copyright © 2023 by Guideposts. All rights reserved.

This book, or parts thereof, may not be reproduced, stored in a retrieval system, or transmitted in any form or by any means, electronic, mechanical, photocopying, recording, or otherwise, without the written permission of the publisher.

This is a work of fiction. While the setting of Mercy Hospital as presented in this series is fictional, the location of Charleston, South Carolina, actually exists, and some places and characters may be based on actual places and people whose identities have been used with permission or fictionalized to protect their privacy. Apart from the actual people, events, and locales that figure into the fiction narrative, all other names, characters, businesses, and events are the creation of the author's imagination and any resemblance to actual persons or events is coincidental.

Every attempt has been made to credit the sources of copyrighted material used in this book. If any such acknowledgment has been inadvertently omitted or miscredited, receipt of such information would be appreciated.

Scripture references are from the following sources: *The Holy Bible, King James Version* (KJV). *The Holy Bible, New International Version* (NIV). Copyright © 1973, 1978, 1984, 2011 by Biblica, Inc. Used by permission of Zondervan. All rights reserved worldwide. www.zondervan.com.

Cover and interior design by Müllerhaus
Cover illustration by Bob Kayganich at Illustration Online LLC.
Typeset by Aptara, Inc.

This book was previously published under the title *Merciful Secrecy* as part of the *Miracles & Mysteries of Mercy Hospital* series.

ISBN 978-1-959634-50-8 (hardcover)
ISBN 978-1-959634-52-2 (epub)
ISBN 978-1-959634-51-5 (epdf)

Printed and bound in the United States of America
10 9 8 7 6 5 4 3 2 1

MERCIFUL SECRECY

 Chapter One

ANNE MABRY HAD HER HANDS full as she hurried through the main entrance of Mercy Hospital. Full of cookies, that is.

An early April breeze followed her up the front walk. Not stiff enough to wreak havoc with her hair, but with enough *oomph* to remind Anne that while winter was over, spring in Charleston could bring its share of unpleasant surprises. But not today.

Today she brought fancy boxes of pastel-frosted cookies for her friends, not for any special reason. Just because. Of course, Easter was coming. It was late this year, and folks would have garden flowers tucked in, while early perennials would bob their heads. Her daughter Lili was stateside again, and she and Ralph would be celebrating the holiday with their daughter and granddaughter.

A wonderful end of the Lenten season, made even brighter with the surprise of freshly frosted sugar cookies.

She slipped one container onto the records desk, rang the little bell, and then offered her good friend Evelyn Perry a cheerful wave as she hurried back the other way. She slipped the next box onto the counter alongside the gift shop cash register where her friend Joy Atkins worked. Joy had lived in Charleston just over a year and had been hired at Mercy to shape up the outdated gift shop. Being Joy and Texan, she also managed to charm folks with her thick drawl and warm manner.

Anne glanced at her watch.

She had just enough time to get a third box over to Nurse Shirley Bashore in the ER. Shirley floated as needed, but right now she was assigned to the emergency room. The ER crew was sizable, so their box was bigger than the others.

Anne hurried down the sloping, wheelchair-friendly floor and popped through the automated sliding glass doors. The doors separated the busy emergency room from the recently renovated lobby and second-floor mezzanine overlooking the inviting main entrance.

She'd been here a long time. Over thirty years now, and she'd watched the hospital grow and change and expand in multiple ways. Why, it was—

She stopped in her tracks as she rounded the corner to the centralized ER nursing station.

The curtained cubicles were a blend of sounds, but that wasn't what forced her to hit the brakes. It was the worried expression on Shirley's face from whatever Katie McNamara—a young ER nurse—was saying.

Anne considered a retreat. She didn't want to interrupt important things concerning patients, and timing in the emergency room was everything. She understood that.

And as good as her cookies were, she didn't have to interrupt whatever was being discussed. She started to turn just as Shirley spotted her. She motioned Anne forward, then led both women into a small stockroom. And when the three of them crowded into the glorified closet, Shirley quietly closed the door and turned. Hands on her hips, she met Anne's gaze and indicated Katie with a flick of her thumb. "I think there is someone stalking this young lady, Anne, and I won't be able to rest if we don't put an end to it."

"Stalking?" Anne was still holding the cookies. She handed them to Shirley and turned toward Katie. "Katie, are you sure?"

The blond, blue-eyed nurse made a noncommittal face. "I'm not sure of anything, but I'm kinda scared. It's stupid little stuff happening that doesn't add up. Flowers gone missing from my backyard patio. My car unlocked when I'm sure I locked it. A feeling like I'm being watched, but when I turn around, no one's there. And now this stupid card, stuck under my windshield wiper that says, 'Good morning, Katie.'"

A shiver chased down Anne's spine. "Who would do this?"

Katie shook her head. "I have no idea. I don't have any enemies unless you count Mary Rita Fairbanks. Mary Rita was determined to be named Miss Summer Peach back in our senior year of high school, and rumor had it she was contemplating a contract hit when the judges gave me the title after tasting my peach-and-pecan pie."

"Teen girls are nothing if not dramatic," noted Anne. She knew Katie was kidding, but she believed her when she said she had no enemies. The twenty-seven-year-old ER nurse was known for her kindness to everyone.

"Exactly," Katie drawled. "I didn't see the contest as life-and-death, but it's possible that not winning a costume-jewelry tiara put Mary Rita over the edge. I'm happy to say she is now married with a sweet baby boy and all is forgiven." She was making light of the situation, but Anne read the concern in her eyes.

"I'll take her off the suspect list," declared Anne. She went along with the humor, although she fully intended to delve further into the incidents. On the less serious side, she made a mental note to check out that recipe, because the thought of mixing ripe peaches with crunchy pecans sounded marvelous, any time of year.

Katie chuckled. "That's how far back I've got to go to find anyone who's upset with me. No bad romances. No romance to speak of for a while, actually. Kitty Sue and I were discussing the lack of current opportunity the other day."

Kitty Sue had come on board as an ER nurse the year before. Because she was blond and blue-eyed like Katie, people often got the two young women mixed up. Katie rolled her eyes. "Being short-staffed here has kept me too busy to even think about dating, and my mother is sure that work is thwarting any chance she might have to become a grandmother while she's young enough to enjoy it. She reminds me of that every time she sends me links for dating sites. When I remind her that I'm being patient, she reminds me that a girl can only be patient for so long."

"As someone who's also kept her mother waiting, that's a conversation I understand all too well," said Shirley.

"Green-eyed monsters grabbed hold of my mother about the time my cousin Ro got married two years back." Katie made a face that made Anne smile. "My lagging behind has been my mother's main theme since then."

"I've got friends from church on a similar time frame," noted Anne. "First to the altar. First to the nursery. Then the first to be potty-trained, as if toileting is a skill of grand intelligence."

"Exactly. And Ro just announced her pregnancy, so Mama is after me to cut back hours to allow for a social life. Or find a nice eligible doctor."

"You're in a target-rich environment for that." Anne grinned, teasing, although she'd seen a couple of interesting looks pass between the hardworking nurse and their head of security, but maybe she'd been assuming too much.

"And I was just about to start hunting one down when these weird things began happening," Katie quipped. "Thwarted again."

Katie wasn't one to go off the deep end over anything, and that was part of what made her a stellar emergency room nurse. Despite that and her humor just now, Anne read the worry in her eyes.

"Well, that peach-and-pecan pie sounds marvelous, and I bet my mama would love the recipe, but right now we need to think about keeping Katie safe," said Shirley. The experienced fortysomething nurse had moved back to Charleston from Atlanta the year before when her mother began showing signs of mental wear. Happily, Regina's acuity seemed better now that Shirley was here.

"It was the year before they gave home ec the ax, so I'm possibly the last of my kind," said Katie. "A dying breed. Which is a terrible choice of words if this is, indeed, a stalker."

"Girl, do not even joke about such a thing." Shirley scolded. Her gleaming dark eyes reflected her worry.

"Katie, when did this start?" Anne asked.

Shirley's pager buzzed. She took a deep breath and reached for the door. "I've got to get on the floor. I'm due in at eight, and it's five till now."

"Talk later?" Anne asked as Shirley swung open the door.

"I'm done at four. So is Katie."

"I'm done at three," Anne replied. "Addie is working on a Lenten project with a couple of kids from church, so she won't get dropped off until five or so, and Ralph is on supper duty because Lili is working late on base. Can the three of us meet at four?"

"My grandpa is coming by to pick me up," Katie said. "He's taking me out for supper on the water, but I can have him come a little later."

"You arrange that, and we'll see what we can figure out," Anne told her. "Shirley, does that work for you? Is your mom okay on her own for a little longer?"

"Mama is loving these longer days of spring," Shirley assured her. "She's much more active and gets out more."

Anne smiled. "That's so good to hear." Regina's improvement was a blessing, for sure, but as Anne hurried back to the front desk, worry plagued her. There had been an uptick in crimes recently in Charleston. Not around the hospital she loved, per se, but not all that far from it, and she'd heard the concern in Katie's voice.

Good morning, Katie.

The note under the windshield had made it personal.

She used the hour between when her shift ended and when she was meeting the gals to grab an afternoon sweet tea and head out to the angel statue.

She took a seat at a nearby bench and looked up.

The Angel of Mercy had a special place in the hearts of hospital workers and patients. The angel had earned her spot in the beautifully landscaped garden leading to the Grove, the dedicated green space that connected the hospital, its new wings, and professional buildings with a network of walkways. And it was here that Anne had offered up many a prayer over the years.

The beautiful weather had inspired activity. People were strolling along East Bay. Streams of folks were walking every which way through the Grove, and the front of the hospital was always busy during the day, folks coming and going. Anne was used to this. She'd learned long ago how to ignore the activity and focus on prayer.

What she couldn't ignore was her concern for the young nurse, so she didn't wait the full hour before heading toward the ER entrance on the waterfront side of the building.

Fresh air bathed her in the essence of spring. She breathed it in, but as she rounded the corner to cut across the grass to beeline it for the ER, she paused.

A man was tucked in the curve of the bushes. To his right was the Emergency Room entrance. On his left was a columnar yew, one of the tall ones, just big enough that he would be pretty much unnoticed unless one happened to cut across the lawn just so.

And it wasn't just his positioning that made Anne slip her phone out and snap a silent picture.

It was the way he studied the twin doorways and the nearby ambulance entrance, as if watching for something.

Or someone.

He looked familiar. Kind of.

Not like friend familiar, but as if she'd seen him around. Around here? The church? The neighborhood?

She didn't know.

He didn't look her way as she continued across the grass. And sure enough, when she got to the double doors, he wasn't visible. And yet she knew he was there. Watching. Waiting.

The cold thread snaked its way up her back again. She darted through the doors, and when Katie and Shirley came her way a few minutes later, she motioned toward an empty alcove of the waiting room.

"It's too lovely outside to waste another minute indoors, isn't it?" Shirley's longing gaze matched her tone. "How about we take a seat at one of the picnic tables in the Grove?"

Anne didn't want to heighten their concerns, and the older man lurking in the bushes might have nothing to do with Katie McNamara's plight, but she wanted to err on the side of caution. "Blame it on the sun or whatever, but this works better for me right now. If that's all right?"

Shirley shrugged. "Well, in that case, of course." The three women tucked themselves into a back corner table of the sequestered area. In busy times, this small area was packed full of people, but today they had plenty of room in the main waiting area that surrounded the triage desk.

"We have to figure out how to proceed." Anne kept her voice soft in case anyone came in. "I don't think Katie should be alone, especially if she's working a late shift. There's a reason most crime happens at night."

Katie shivered. "Well, I was only mildly concerned before. I'm about to go to full-fledged fright if you keep this up."

"Y'all know how I love my mysteries," Anne reminded them. She loved reading them, particularly British ones. The dry humor was right up her alley. "Sometimes a healthy fear makes us more aware, and that's not always a bad thing. I say we go to the police."

Katie made a face. "Who will roll their eyes and tell me I'm making a big deal out of nothing."

"Which of course you aren't," argued Shirley. "From a perfectly normal existence a week ago, to three things happening in the past few days…"

Anne pulled out her phone and opened her notepad app. "There was nothing suspicious prior to this?"

"Livin' the dream," drawled Katie, grinning. "I love my job, and even though I complain about the lack of eligible men around here, I don't fret over that until Mama sends a text."

Shirley laughed. "I hear you."

"I've racked my brain trying to figure out if I crossed someone, or if there was a patient who seemed overly interested in me, or someone on social media, and there's nothing," she assured them. "Nothing at all."

"Except Mrs. Spencer," said Shirley.

Katie winced. "It can't be her. Do you think?"

"Who's Mrs. Spencer?" asked Anne.

"Lee Spencer," replied Shirley. "She lost her husband about six months back. His heart gave out at work, and they brought him in when Katie was on. It was a busy Friday right before Halloween, and he didn't make it."

Katie sighed. "She blamed me for not getting the doctor to him in time."

"She threatened Katie," noted Shirley, and when Katie made a face, Shirley folded her arms. "She did, and that's a fact. I know things are said in anger and grief, but that woman was out of line. She wrote letters to the administration and to Dr. Barnhardt, and she's been threatening a lawsuit even though there was no fault involved. Still, when folks are dealing with that much grief and anger it's hard to not want to find someone to blame."

"Grief is a tough master," agreed Anne.

"I know it's unlikely," Shirley said to Katie, "but we need to consider all possibilities." She bit her lower lip as she stood up. "We'll walk you to your car—"

"It's broad daylight." Skepticism tinged the young woman's voice and hiked her brows. "I'm pretty sure I'll be okay."

"Humor us. I'm not about to spend my life wondering 'what if I'd walked Katie to her car that day?' Uh-uh." Shirley slung her bag up over her arm as she led the way to the double doors. "We may not know much right now, but we know enough to be on guard, and that's something." She went through the doors first. Katie and Anne followed. And just as they began the walk toward the ER parking lot, a man came their way.

The same man Anne had seen in the bushes a quarter hour before, and he was looking at them—right at them—intently.

She called Shirley's name softly.

Shirley hiked on, blissfully unaware.

Anne took hold of Katie's arm, not so softly. "This way." She tugged Katie toward the grass.

Katie resisted.

"This way. Now," Anne ordered softly. The man was drawing closer. Much closer. And he was moving in quickly.

Anne didn't make eye contact with him. Eyes down, she moved off the path.

Shirley kept right on walking, her bag swinging with each step, ready to go home and enjoy the rest of the day. Suddenly she turned to say something and spotted Anne tugging Katie to the side. "Girls, which way are we going? What are you—"

"Katie-girl!" The man's voice—sounding cheerful and normal, much to Anne's surprise—broke in.

Katie slipped away from Anne's grasp. "Gramps! Thanks for meeting me."

Anne lifted her gaze as Katie threw her arms around the man.

He hugged her back. And when he did, Anne read the worry in his features, as if he was holding a most precious gift.

But why was he worried?

And more importantly...

Why was he hiding in the bushes? What did he know?

Katie kept her arm tucked in his as she turned. "Anne, this is my grandpa, Liam Holden. He moved down here from Atlanta when he retired from being the world's best detective for the Atlanta PD."

Anne started to greet him, but Katie's words brought Shirley back their way.

"Detective Holden." Shirley's brows shifted up as she closed the few steps between them. "We met in Atlanta, several times. I was in the ER at Emory."

"And always willing to help the police." Liam Holden held out a hand and shook Shirley's. "It's nice to see you again, Nurse. And to know you're here with our Katie."

"Well, she is an absolute treasure to work with," Shirley declared, smiling. "You two go on and have a nice dinner. The water is still as glass right now, perfect for a quiet night. Katie, I'll see you in the morning."

"First thing," Katie promised. She hesitated as if wanting to say more, but didn't. She smiled instead, looped her arm through her grandfather's, and headed toward the parking lot.

Shirley started to follow them.

Anne caught her arm. "Stay here a minute," she whispered.

Shirley paused.

Katie got into her grandpa's car. She left hers in the lot, presumably to pick it up later, and when they'd circled the drive toward the exit, Anne finally breathed.

"What are we waiting for?" whispered Shirley.

Anne shook her head. "I don't know, but I do know one thing. The first person we check out will be Liam, because normal grandfathers don't hide in the bushes, watching the entrance to hospitals. Even grandfathers who are former detectives. Why was he hiding and taking pictures?" She pulled out her phone and showed Shirley the photo she'd taken.

Shirley's jaw went slack. "That's him, all right. He was well-known in Atlanta, one of those guys who dogged a case until he brought folks to justice. What a coincidence that he's Katie's grandpa, he's living here, and he's hiding in bushes." Her expression said it might not be a coincidence at all, and Anne was inclined to agree.

"I say we contact Detective Holden tomorrow. We're meeting Joy and Evelyn at the café for our usual Tuesday morning coffee, right?"

"Yes."

"I'll text them to meet thirty minutes sooner."

"Evelyn will kill you."

Anne laughed as she began the text right then and there. "But then she'll forgive me if we have a steaming hot coffee waiting for her. And a puzzle. You know how Evelyn likes loose ends tied up and everything in proper order."

"That's Evelyn, for certain."

"Well, there's nothing proper about a young woman being stalked and a grandpa hiding in bushes, so let's bring the others up to speed before we approach Detective Holden. I'll ask him to come at our normal time. That way we'll have a chance to discuss what we want to say to him."

"Perfect."

It was a solid plan, but Anne needn't have worried. When she hurried up Water Street to meet her friends the next morning, Liam Holden was waiting there, and he didn't leave a moment to wonder why. He came forward swiftly. Anne couldn't miss the worried crease of the man's brow as Shirley approached and Joy exited the café carrying their tray of hot drinks. He swept the three of them a look, then splayed his hands. "I'm Liam Holden, Katie McNamara's grandfather," he said to Evelyn as she approached. "I need help, ladies. Serious help. I can't go to the police like I would normally, for reasons I'll explain later, but you gals have a reputation for seeing things. Figuring things out. Noticing." The worry in his voice didn't just capture Anne's attention. All four women listened intently as the retired detective continued. "I'm afraid someone might try to harm my granddaughter, my beautiful Katie, and I'm pretty sure…" His voice broke, and his eyes grew moist. "It's all my fault."

Chapter Two

EVEN OUTSIDE, GINGER AND BUD'S café was far too busy to carry on a serious conversation about danger. Scads of people streamed in and out of the popular café and bakery in the morning hours, and unobtrusive cell phones caught too many private moments these days. Anne handed out the drinks. "We've got just enough time for a quick conference around the corner. Come with us. Please." She had a mile-long list to accomplish between patients and hospital tasks today. But Liam Holden's confession just bumped Katie's safety to number one on the list.

They gathered under a grove of newly leafed trees between the hospital and the waterfront. The later opening of nearby professional buildings afforded them shade and privacy. "Here." Anne handed Liam her own coffee. "Robust Bayside blend with a splash of cream," she explained. "I gave up fancy coffees for Lent. Sometimes simple is best. Now tell us what's going on."

"Should we start with introductions?" Ever-calm Shirley posed the question with a wry expression.

"Of course." Anne perched on the edge of a picnic table after checking for unwanted deposits. The wide-planked table was under a big, leafy tree, after all, and birds were prevalent. "Evelyn, Joy, this is Katie McNamara's grandfather, Liam Holden. He and Shirley met when he was a detective in Atlanta. She was working the ER at Emory. Liam, this is Evelyn Perry from Mercy's records department and Joy Atkins, who runs the gift shop."

"Small world," Evelyn said quietly.

"Smaller yet to realize my granddaughter was working here with Nurse Bashore," noted Liam.

"Shirley," she said.

He took a breath. "Shirley," he repeated. "Look, I know you've all got to get to work, so let me give you a quick rundown. Katie's adopted."

The women exchanged looks. "Okay." Shirley's tone said there must be more.

There was.

"It was a private adoption," he said. "Perfectly legal. My daughter wasn't able to have children. That was bad enough, but then they had an adoption rescinded at the last minute, just days before the judge was going to grant the permanent seal of adoption. They had to relinquish their little boy back to his birth mother."

"What a heartbreak for everyone," Joy whispered.

"It was. They'd had him for five months, and they were over the moon in love with that little fellow. Theo," he added. "Named for my father. It was hard on Sunny," he explained. "That's my daughter. Sunny McNamara. She's a wonderful and accomplished woman, but losing Theo was almost her undoing. I didn't think she was going to get over it. She didn't want to try adoption again, and she was out of options. She seemed defeated. But then a lawyer got hold of me. He had a unique case, a little girl who needed an adoptive home because her father was entering a witness protection program. He gave his little girl up so that no one would be able to track her down."

Anne whistled lightly. "That's true sacrificial love."

"It sure is," said Shirley. "So why do you think she's in danger, Liam?"

"I still have friends in the department in Atlanta," he told them. "I received a call a few days ago from one of my old colleagues who said someone had been asking questions about this little girl. Just a few hours later Katie told me that she felt like someone was watching her. She said it gave her the creeps."

Anne frowned. "Did they know who'd been asking questions?"

He shook his head. "No. Someone called once, and they received a couple of emails. Nothing in person. Which means the person doesn't want to be recognized or traced. Let me just add that the testimony of Katie's father was crucial in sending two killers to jail for life twenty-five years ago, but they didn't act alone. They're part of a crime family that deals in all kinds of bad stuff in and around Atlanta, and they vowed vengeance. I promise you, they meant it."

"You think they've found Katie?"

"I can't sleep for thinking it," he said. "We left nothing open, and Sunny and her husband have always kept the few details they know to themselves, but last night Katie told me she'd sent a cheek swab to a DNA registry site and requested links to any possible relatives. She thinks it's a lark," he said, choking up. "In reality it could be a death sentence."

"Because if she's related to people on the site—" Evelyn began.

"And if someone mentions it or reaches out—" added Shirley.

"Then Katie gets found with a target on her back," Anne finished the awful thought. "Does Katie have any idea there could be bad guys out to get her?"

"No. We were always open about the adoption but no details. I made sure everything was sealed up tight. Sunny and Drake don't even have all the facts behind this. They only know that the father gave Katie up after losing his wife and then witnessing the crime."

"Forgive me for asking, but is a grieving man cognizant enough to have made a decision like that?" asked Evelyn.

"God's timing, ma'am." Liam Holden spoke plainly. "There was nothing we could do to mitigate the timing for the father. I never met him personally. The department kept him tucked away until the trial, and he testified against the mob family about fifteen months later. By then Katie had been with my daughter and son-in-law for nearly a year. It all happened quickly on the father's side. When he realized the full impact of what his testimony would do, he instigated the contact with the adoption attorney. Katie's biological father wasn't involved in the crimes, but he was savvy enough about the Malloy family to know he was a marked man forever. There was no way he wanted his daughter to carry that stigma with her, only now—"

Liam Holden wasn't a tall man, but he carried himself tall. Strong. Square-shouldered. He paused to take a breath, and when he began again his voice was strong but his shoulders slumped. "Something's in the air. A smart girl like Katie knows when things are off-kilter, and it doesn't take a fancy degree to know how things are linked on ancestry sites. She doesn't know who she's related to, but the mob does, and after thirty years of dealing with mob mentality, let me assure you of this." He squared his shoulders again and leaned in. "They never forget, and they never forgive. Blood for blood."

An icy chill grabbed Anne despite the beautiful spring day. "We need to go to the police, Liam. We have to. I—"

"We can't," he told her frankly. "I'd like to say the mob has no influence in police circles, but it would be a lie. All you need is one informant who is either owned by the mob for whatever reason, or a dirty cop that likes mob pay as a side job, and my girl winds up dead."

The icy chill deepened, and Anne pulled her sweater closer. "Here? In Charleston?"

"I was on the inside for a long time," he told her. "You might have 98 percent great cops, but it only takes one of the 2 percent to get their hands on information and sell it off. I'll help protect her, but I can't be around 24/7, and I can't be here at Mercy nonstop or she'll get worried."

"And she's understandably concerned now," said Shirley.

Anne stood. "Ladies, let's meet to talk about this after work."

"My place," said Joy. "We don't dare discuss this inside the hospital."

"Four o'clock?"

All four women agreed, then Shirley turned to Liam. "I'll text you so you have my contact information."

Liam offered his cell phone number.

The three other women then texted Liam.

That way he had their names and numbers.

They had his.

"We've got to clock in," Evelyn reminded them. "Liam, thank you for sharing your information with us. Give us time to talk things over this afternoon."

"And we'll get back to you with our thoughts," said Anne.

"All I can ask," he replied then walked away.

The women exchanged looks.

There was nothing more to add. Not right now. But Anne saw her concern reflected on the three other faces. As she hurried to the main lobby, she wondered if this time they might be in over their heads.

Mob? Witness protection?

Yesterday she passed out pastel-frosted cookies.

Today she pondered a potential hit on an innocent colleague, and while she understood Liam's reticence about going straight to the police, there was no way the women could do this alone. Or even contemplate it. Why—

Her pager went off with a code she'd hoped she'd never see.

CODE ORANGE. SEEK SECURE SHELTER IMMEDIATELY.

Code Orange meant an active shooter in the hospital.

Anne's heart jumped. Her fingertips buzzed with an adrenaline boost, but she knew what to do.

She put her heart on "steady" with a firm dose of faith. Hospital security had trained all the front desk personnel on how to respond. They were actually among the first to be trained because a hospital lobby was the core of a bi-level web extending in every direction with multiple doorways.

Phones pinged around her as incoming staff received a similar message. The code sent people scurrying for shelter.

Forcing a calm she didn't feel, Anne gathered up two elderly women, one therapy dog and its trainer, and a family of three and directed them into the gift shop.

Joy opened the door for them, then shut it quickly as the lobby emptied. She turned the lock firmly as Anne ushered the confused folks into the back room behind the quaint shop.

"Coffee's fresh, everyone." Nonplussed, Joy pointed to the tray of creamers and sweetening packets. The small room held shelves of back stock, a narrow desktop barely bigger than the laptop it held, a desk chair, and a couple of boxes. Since Joy had come on board at the gift shop, she kept fresh coffee on hand to offer to first responders and folks just needing a quick lift of kindness. The fresh coffee seemed welcome right now.

"What's happening? Why are we here?" asked the father of the young family.

"Protocol," Anne told him. "We got a code on our phones, and we have to follow protocol until we get an all clear. It's usually not long, but this is where one sector of the lobby comes when we need to seek shelter."

"But the weather's clear as can be," protested one of the older women. "And it's stuffy in here. The air's downright heavy."

"Weather's still clear," said the mother of the young family as she waved her phone.

The therapy dog owner exchanged a look with Anne then added a calming comment. "You know how it is. Things happen, alarms go off, and everyone follows the drill. And how wonderful to know that Mercy Hospital is so well prepared, Anne."

"Practice drills keep us ready for anything," agreed Anne. But if there was an active shooter in the hospital, she didn't feel one bit ready. And yet she'd done exactly what she'd been trained to do, and when Joy closed the door to the back room and flipped the lock into place, the family moved closer together. So did the elderly women. One of them swallowed hard, then reached into her purse and pulled out a deck of cards. She held it out to the young couple's little boy. "Do you play cards?"

"With my grampa."

"What's your favorite game?"

"Old Maid."

The other elderly woman laughed, but the first one just smiled and handed the boy the cards. "You good for a game?"

"Maybe." He looked at his mom and dad.

They nodded.

"'Kay."

Joy moved the laptop, and the pair got to play a full game before the "all clear" was sounded on Anne's pager.

She was near the door. When the tone came through, she unlocked the door and swung it open. A welcome rush of gift shop cool air flooded the room.

The dog woofed.

One by one the folks gathered their purses or bags and moved back to the lobby.

"I told you," the young mother said to no one in particular. "Not a cloud in the sky."

Her husband palmed their son's head. "Maybe moved north or south. I'm just happy it's all good so we don't have to reschedule Brian's procedure."

A nurse called their name right then. She ushered them down the hall as if nothing had happened. Anne hoped that was the case.

She turned to the woman with the cards. "Thank you for stepping in like you did. That was really nice of you."

"My pleasure. I've always got a deck at hand. My mama raised us to play cards, and I've kept it up for over seventy years. Now that's a useful legacy."

Anne grinned. "It sure is."

The women moved toward the coffee kiosk across the way. Anne turned toward the dog trainer. "Thank you."

The woman shrugged it off. "Brandy has never been part of a drill like that, so it was good to see how she'd react to being put in an unfamiliar situation. She did all right."

"She sure did."

The lobby filled as quickly as it had cleared, and, per protocol, the staff didn't gather and whisper about what happened. Not in the open.

Anne took comfort knowing that if something bad had happened, they'd be apprised, so for this moment no news was good news. Still, the thought of an active shooter took her right back to Katie's situation. She texted Shirley when she got a chance. ALL CLEAR THERE?

100%.

Anne wanted to ask more, but she forced herself to tuck the phone away and get to work. An hour later a staff-wide message came through. FALSE ALARM. SYSTEM MALFUNCTION. THANK YOU FOR HANDLING THE SITUATION LIKE THE PROFESSIONALS YOU ARE.

Relief flooded her. For nearly ninety minutes she hadn't been able to get the thought of someone hunting Katie out of her mind. A system mess-up was a much better alternative.

The morning flew by, but the false alarm had clarified something for her.

Katie's safety wasn't something the four women could handle alone. She understood Liam's reticence about involving police, but Mercy wasn't just a hospital anymore. Over the years it had become a complex of centers and professional buildings, overseen by a solid security crew. And leading that crew was Seamus McCord, as trustworthy a man as you could find. It only made sense to bring him on board.

Chapter Three

Charleston, South Carolina
1967

"Angel of God, my Guardian dear, to whom God's love commits me here. Ever this day be at my side, to light and guard, to rule and guide."

The beautiful words filled Susie Stanton's heart. Their long-awaited dream—a dream come true—was only weeks away. The child she and Hollis had longed for was soon to be born, and her heart couldn't be fuller or happier.

She held up the intricately embroidered wall hanging. The seven women sighed their admiration accordingly as Susie read the sweet poem out loud. Then she faced the woman whose tender loving care had helped raise her when her own mother went home to Jesus. "I will cherish this forever, Miss Molly. It's so pretty. And it will be perfect on the baby's wall."

"And done in all colors, so it don't matter if it's a boy or a girl," Molly Abernathy replied. "It just matters that it's for a precious child of God," she went on. "Like you were to your mama back in the day. And still are to all of us today!" She laughed. "Land sakes, I didn't mean to make it sound like you weren't still special, Susie-Cusie."

The childhood nickname made Susie smile.

"It's lovely, Molly." Susie's aunt Ellie took the pretty hanging and passed it around. Each woman admired the perfectly placed stitches, and their praise made Molly sit straighter and taller.

Susie's late mother had been Ellie's younger sister, and Ellie had insisted on throwing the baby shower. She'd even had her husband, Ronald, put a fresh coat of paint on the walls.

Ronald was a smoker. Not a casual smoker, but a one-right-after-the-other type, and the walls had yellowed more than a little over the years. Ellie promised Susie fresh white walls to frame the shower. That's what Loretta would have expected, she'd said. Losing Loretta had been a surprise to everyone. Generally speaking, folks didn't die from heart attacks at such a young age.

Loretta was the exception to the rule.

"Molly." Candace Affleck owned the house next door to Ellie. Susie had been friends with Candace's girls forever. The girls weren't here though. DeeDee was working on Folly Beach, and Lainey had gotten herself one of those good jobs at the women's college upriver, and they were still in session. "Did you do this whole thing freehand?"

Candace asked. "Saints be praised, woman, that handwriting is perfect. I don't know that I can breathe proper with that much talent in the room."

"My mama's handwritin'," Molly explained. "And much like her mama's before her. Funny how a body can pass down somethin' like that, ain't it? When I was young I thought it all chance, one thing bein' like another, but the older I get, and the more family lines I see, the clearer it gets that there's somethin' goin' on inside us. Oh, I don't mean that somethin' that says you're gonna have that hair color and those teeth. It's more than that, because how else could you explain a thirstin' for knowledge, or a leanin' toward medicine, or three women havin' the same handwritin' over sixty years of time? Sixty-plus, actually." Molly lifted her narrow shoulders. She wasn't big. Never had been. But her slim frame had provided care for dozens of folks over the years. And probably more that Susie knew nothing about, because Molly wasn't one to toot her own horn.

The elderly woman had been a loving presence in her life. Molly had been a close friend to Susie's mother and grandmother, and when Loretta's heart gave out, Molly had stepped into the void. Most folks thought it should be Aunt Ellie's place, but Susie knew better. Aunt Ellie was nice enough. She tried to be kind, but Uncle Ronald wouldn't want to be paying the way for anyone's child, so when Molly stepped up, Susie was pretty sure her aunt had breathed a huge sigh of relief.

Molly had no money. But no one cared about that.

And Molly's clothes were straight out of a 1940s ragbag, castoffs given to St. Andrew's annual clothing drive, where volunteers got first pick.

No one cared about that either.

They didn't care, because Molly had the biggest heart of all. She didn't have the stuff most folks wanted, because she gave it away. "Always someone 'at needs it more'n we do," she'd tell Susie. She was a woman who put love first and foremost.

And she was right—mostly.

Although they both still regretted her decision not to buy the white dress all the girls at Crichton Academy were wearing for graduation. Not wanting to put pressure on folks during tough times, the principal had made it clear that white was an option. Not a decree.

Molly took that to mean the other graduates would be picking their own best colors for the class of 1963.

No, ma'am.

Susie Standish was the standout in the crowd, because while she wore a muted blue lace dress—freshly dyed by Molly to cover the faded stain on one side—all one hundred and four of the other girls wore white.

She'd buried the humiliation because Molly would never intentionally hurt or embarrass her.

But it stung. It stung deep. Susie vowed then that if she ever had a child, that child would be raised as normal as anyone has ever been raised. Because there were good—and not so good—ways to stand out.

"What made you think of this sweet poem, Molly?" Celia Bennett handed the pretty embroidery off to her left as she posed the question.

"I live in a land of angels," Molly replied.

The women went a little bit quiet. Enough so they all could hear.

"From my mama and her mama and her mama, the thought of angels lookin' down on us, lookin' after us, bein' right here beside us has always been important to us." Molly sat back and sighed. She'd lost several of her bottom teeth over the years, but the loss didn't diminish her smile. She flashed it, bright as ever, letting her aging light shine just so.

"Mama made pictures of angels. Sketched them right out with pencils and paper, and folks loved those reminders that no matter what happens, the Lord's got us. And keeps us. And has His very grace watchin' over us, lookin' out for us. So when I heard this baby was comin', I thought the first thing this child needs is his or her mama and daddy, and the second thing is knowin' a guardian angel's been assigned. And is here. Right here." She beamed a confident smile around the room. "With us, even now. Ready to take charge of this little one, for the Lord is good!"

"Amen to that," Celia replied. "And Molly Abernathy, you don't just have a way with handwriting and stitching. You have a way of putting things right with words, and that's another wonderful blessing."

Molly brought folks together.

No one quite knew how. Or talked about it all that much.

She drew all kinds of folks. Didn't matter their color or their church or the way they tied their shoes, Molly was a friend to all, and she'd brought Susie up with that same mindset.

Molly might patch her own boots by slipping her feet into empty bread bags, but she'd lay two dollars down to get a brand-spankin'-new pair for a child in need. Her grace set that tone, and Susie embraced it 100 percent. They didn't have much, but they had love. And love was enough.

Chapter Four

ANNE WAS WAITING FOR THE silver elevators with a patient who'd just been discharged when Seamus McCord hurried toward Garrison Baker's office at lunchtime. The busy administrator made it a habit to stay in his office, grab a PB&J or two, and fit in meetings and calls he wouldn't otherwise get to.

Garrison Baker was her kind of people.

Seamus didn't pause at Garrison's door. He went right in, and Anne was pretty sure she knew why. She made small talk with her patient as she guided the wheelchair to the pickup loop once they were down on ground level. When the elderly woman was tucked into the back seat of her daughter's SUV, Anne parked the chair and started for the front desk.

She spotted Seamus moving across the mezzanine level above, part of the gorgeous lobby remodel a few years back.

She moved toward the stairs, and when he descended them at a quick clip, she motioned him toward the angel wing hallway. "I know you're busy," she whispered quickly. "But what happened this morning to cause the Code Orange?"

"Nothing I can talk about, Anne. Even the best systems fail at times."

"*Fail* generally means something doesn't happen as planned. In this case, something happened. The alert went out. If you didn't send it, who did?"

"Exactly what I'm trying to find out," he told her.

Anne stared at him. After she'd listened to Liam's story of bad cops and good cops and people imprisoned for life and someone possibly targeting a young colleague, the thought that their protective system wasn't working spiked her pulse. "It's broken?"

"No. It appears to be absolutely fine. Working as needed."

Maybe Anne had been reading too many mysteries, but alert systems that acted on their own generally meant havoc would ensue a few chapters down the line. "Seamus, were we sabotaged?" She swallowed hard around a lump in her throat. "Should we be worried?"

He drew his brows down. His eyes narrowed. "That's a lot of questions, Anne. Why do I sense something else is going on?"

"Because you're suspicious by nature?"

He held her gaze. "I've got to get back to work. I would appreciate it not becoming instant speculation, if at all possible. Although I know people will talk."

He was right. "Will you tell me when you figure things out?"

He lifted one brow in reply.

"So—no."

"Need-to-know basis, Anne. I could tell you…" He paused, and Anne knew the rest of the saying, because Ralph loved great spy movies.

"But then I'd have to kill you." She finished the quote for him. "At least keep me posted about the fixing. Okay?"

He gave her that look again, the look that delved. "We'll chat again."

They would too.

Seamus didn't want anyone hurt, but he was one of those rare guys who respected Anne and her friends' ability to go unnoticed.

A lot of folks tended to clam up when a big, strong, military-cut police type walked into the room, but toss four middle-aged-and-beyond Southern women into the mix and tongues kept wagging. The women weren't above using their personal cloak of invisibility to their advantage.

Anne's shift was done before her friends', and making a trip to Ginger's for something delicious was essential. She counted the walk as exercise, and the justification was clear. Their collective brains worked better with baked goods.

She walked into the café intending to pick up a box of freshly made muffins, but when she spotted Bud's stuffed croissants, she caved. Fresh croissants, baked just enough to be lightly crispy outside, stuffed with chocolate or vanilla custard, whipped cream, and freshly sliced strawberries, were too amazing to pass up. She quietly promised herself more willpower on the following day and ordered six with barely a twinge of conscience.

As Ginger rang her up, the café owner leaned closer and posed a question. "Everyone's talking about the hospital alert this morning, Anne."

She winced.

"They're saying the staff reacted perfectly, but there are more than a few wondering how a shooter alert went out with no shooter."

"Whereas I'm grateful it was nothing," Anne told her. "And glad that no one around the lobby panicked. That was good."

"It was," admitted Ginger, but then she sighed. "A couple of the doctors were talking." She lowered her voice although the café wasn't busy at this time of day. "Wondering if someone was testing the system. You know. To study response time."

"Well, that's a pretty sophisticated person," Anne told her flat out. "I love our hospital, but who can imagine someone of that caliber targeting us?" She shrugged but couldn't deny that Ginger's words gave her something to share with her friends. "This is why I don't watch scary movies, Ginger. Too much to think about." She winked. "Give me a good old cozy mystery instead."

Ginger laughed. "Agreed. Have a nice afternoon, Anne. Thanks for coming by."

"My pleasure." Anne smiled as she tucked the box of treats into her spring bag. She'd lost her favorite tote the year before, and this new one was all right, but it didn't rank favored status. The handle was too long and the bag somewhat inflexible, and when Anne packed in the morning, she did so for the day. Rigid sides were a guard against bringing too much, and that was an annoyance because Anne liked to overpack.

Her phone jingled her daughter's ringtone as Anne headed toward Joy's house on Queen Street. She could have gone along East Bay, but the quaint, homey settings of Church Street called to her. It beckoned tourists too, as horse-drawn wagonloads of people rolled by, a firm nod to the sweetness of spring. "Lili, hey! How's everything going?"

US Air Force Captain Liliana Mabry was stationed at the joint military base in North Charleston. When Lili was deployed, Ralph and Anne took guardianship of Addie, their eight-year-old granddaughter. Lili was stateside again, so Addie was living with her mother. The elementary school they'd chosen for her was located in the middle of the thirteen-minute drive between Anne and Ralph's house and the major military base. That made the school location convenient to all three of them, and Anne and Ralph loved having an influence in the little girl's life.

"I have discovered so many new things about myself now that I'm back in the States," Lili reported.

Her dry tone made Anne laugh. "Do tell."

"Oh yes," Lili continued. Anne heard base sounds in the background, and she marveled with pride at all her daughter had achieved so far. "I've learned that no one makes mac and cheese like you do," she said. "And that your bubbly water is the best Addie's ever had. Although aluminum cans are bad for the environment."

"Well, there you go. I knew she was a smarty from the get-go!" Anne laughed as she walked along the shaded, historic street. "I'll text you a pic of my bubbly brand. It's the cheapest one they carry at the market, and the only reason I get it is because it seems to settle your father's stomach when it's riled. I will support her contention about the cans, and that new soda place on Ashley has deposit bottles back, the glass ones they re-use, so you know that's an easy fix for our eco-friendly child. But the mac and cheese? Honey, that's straight from the famous blue box, and there isn't a person in this world who can't make that happen easily. Especially not an air force captain."

"I bought the fancy one."

Anne laughed. "With melty cheese? That was your mistake. Our girl is not one bit upscale."

Lili laughed. "I hear you. Okay, I'll get the store brand water, and she'd get a kick out of a soda shop, wouldn't she?"

"Remember when they used to have nickel candy in the tubs at the one by us when you were growing up?"

"I loved that," exclaimed Lili. "I'd save my money and get a sack of candy for a dollar, and that was only twenty-five years ago."

"Old Ernie loved that you'd come skipping in and put down those four quarters."

"He was kind to me."

"He sure was." Sometimes they tiptoed around old memories because Anne had focused too much on appearances back then. As a pastor's wife, she'd felt like Lili's behavior reflected Ralph's abilities.

Of course, nothing was further from the truth with most folks, but it took her a while to realize that kids would be kids. It had created a rift between them for a while. But no more. "Ernie's gone home to God, but I'll never forget what a wonderful neighbor he was. His stories were the best. So now that you've had your comeuppance on boxed mac and cheese, what's next?"

"My commander is setting up the teaching time frame, and I wanted to know if you guys have anything on your calendar that I should know about. If they send me off base to give instruction, Addie might be staying with you, and I didn't want to mess anything up."

"Nice of him to consult you."

"It is. He's one of those people who understands the time crunches of being a single parent. Have you got anything going on in the next few months?"

"Nothing major except helping Evelyn with the hospital museum opening," Anne told her. "She's been wanting this for so long, and I promised that we'd be on hand for whatever she needs, but that's it. Other than that, we're free and happy to have Addie with us."

The gorgeous spire of St. Philip's Church rose into the sky before her as she spoke. The bell tower and curve of the road around the massive church a silent testimony. The thought of making a road curve around a church seemed to mean something. Something good. She turned north on Queen Street. "If you need us, we're there, darling. And I'm so excited to have you home for Easter this year!"

"Me too," Lili agreed. "I can't wait to help with things. I haven't been around to plan anything for so long, so planning Easter dinner with you, going to Holy Week services, having Addie there will all seem perfect. A wonderful way to close out winter. Though I can't complain. Winters here are pretty much over in a flash. So what's going on in the hospital, Mom? Fill me in."

"We've got a situation we're working on. Something different."

"Translation: another mystery. Dangerous?"

"No. Well. Mostly not."

Lili half sighed, half laughed. "Mom, you're supposed to say no. That's the only proper answer to that question. And you don't want to put Dad into cardiac arrest, do you?"

"Your father is a strong man. Strong in body and spirit. He'll do okay. And I don't give him too many details. A good cook knows to blend ingredients with care."

"A dash of this and a dollop of that." Lili drawled that last and laughed.

"You know your dad well." Anne was approaching Joy's house. Climbing roses were just beginning to bloom along the short fence separating Joy's driveway and yard from her neighbor's somewhat noisy but cute pair of dust-mop dogs.

The adorable little fellows refused to obey the rules of invisible fencing, so their owners had erected a short, gated, wrought iron fence along the property lines. They'd had to get city approval because no one got to do their own thing in the historic sections of town. The stately and simple fence worked, and the centered gate allowed them access to Joy, and her to them, but kept Bodie and Boppy where they belonged. "Gotta go, honey. Was there a reason for this call? Or just to confirm my mac and cheese total world domination?"

"That—and just to talk."

"I love you, Lili."

Lili laughed. "Me too. We'll come over on Saturday, okay? Do some grilling? Unless Dad's going to get the smoker out and throw some real barbecue together?"

That sounded good. Real good. "I'll look into that," Anne said. "I've got a brisket that would make fine weekend fare."

"And you know I can't get enough Southern barbecue when I'm home," Lili replied. She never complained about deployments or even talked too much about them, but she enjoyed splashes of good old Southern life and cooking when she was at the joint base. "See you Saturday. And good job not asking about my love life, Mom."

"I know better," declared Anne. "I'm trusting that an accomplished woman like you can make up her own mind about prospects. Especially in a target-rich environment like the base."

"A lot of youngsters here, Mom. Not as many thirty- or forty-somethings as there used to be. I might have missed my chance."

"Except with God, everything is possible."

"And that's where we'll leave it," Lili replied. "Love you!"

"Love you too."

Anne tucked the phone away as her three friends approached. Shirley normally carpooled to and from work, but today Anne would take her home. Her car was parked in a lot midway between the hospital complex and Joy's house. She walked forward to meet them at the sidewalk and held out the bakery box. "I brought temptation to bring all y'all around to my way of thinking."

"I love a good dessert bribe," declared Shirley.

"Me too." Joy smiled. She had the gentlest nature of the four, but Anne had gotten to know her well enough to see the gritty lining beneath the genteel presence. "And that's not a muffin box. You've got pastries."

"I tried to resist them," Anne said. "Then I realized we've got to do something radical tomorrow morning, so the thought of coercive food seemed wise."

Joy unlocked the door, and they all moved inside. The coolness of the apartment wasn't from AC. Not yet. Shade trees lining the street spared the front of Joy's home from the sun's intensity. They moved to the kitchen, where late-afternoon light tipped dancing rainbows onto the cupboards and wall.

"Addie would go bonkers over that." Anne indicated the moving shapes as she slit the tape on the bakery box and lifted the lid.

"Those are from the wind chimes and prisms on my porch," said Joy. "Someone asked me once about a side porch facing a thin little driveway like mine, as if what's the point, and I told her that it isn't always about the lookin'. Sometimes it's just about the sittin' and takin' a breath."

"You have a way with words," noted Shirley.

Anne motioned to the box. "I got a croissant for your mom too, Shirley, even though she's at home. I didn't want her to feel left out. And Ralph, of course."

Joy withdrew four flowery plates from the nearby cupboard. "Pretty calls for pretty," she said when Anne eyed the fancy china. "Those pastries will taste even better with these."

Anne wouldn't have thought so, but by the time they were halfway through their overly stuffed croissants, she couldn't disagree.

She didn't wait for everyone to finish before she offered her idea. "I don't know about the rest of you, but when that code came through so early this morning, the only thing I could think of was Katie. That someone was after her."

"Right," Evelyn said. "I can't deny that I thought the same thing."

"I was so glad to find out it was a false alarm," added Joy. "One worry gone. Good!"

"It made me realize that we need to fill Seamus in about what's going on with Katie. For two reasons," she went on. "First, because his job is hospital security, and if we suspect something odd might be happening or could happen at the hospital, he deserves to know. The second reason is just as vital. We need eyes. Seeing how easily Katie's grandfather could be out of sight because of a well-placed and slightly overgrown yew, I realized that the sprawl of the hospital's layout offers a lot of hidden corners and paths. When I first started volunteering at Mercy, a lot of this development was a pipe dream."

Evelyn nodded. It was Evelyn who had coaxed Anne into giving hospital volunteerism a try, and she hadn't looked back since.

"Things were fairly straightforward then, but now the complex stretches out in so many directions, and each one allows another hiding spot."

"And Seamus has cameras." Joy made the simple observation as she lifted her mug.

"Exactly."

"Will Liam be all right about sharing this information?" asked Shirley. "Whatever is going on here, the thought of dirty cops and old crimes and revenge sounds like a Saturday-night movie I wouldn't watch. I don't want Liam or Katie or anyone targeted because word gets out. But you're right, we can't be everywhere."

"I agree." Evelyn tapped her mug of tea lightly. "And Anne has nailed the logistics of the situation. We're all working. Even with Shirley in the ER right now, she can't be around Katie all the time, and the shifts vary, so I don't see a choice. We bring Seamus on board, and that way he and his crew can keep an eye on things. We can let Liam know what we've decided. He did ask for our help."

"We know Seamus." Anne didn't want to introduce a variable but felt it was necessary. "What about the other security guys? We know some of them, but the ones monitoring the cameras are behind the scenes, and I'm a little nervous about too many people being involved."

"Seamus will gloss it over."

Everyone looked at Evelyn, who lifted her mug and peered at them over the rim. "You don't get to be head of security for a place like Mercy Hospital without understanding how to get the job done in the least obtrusive way possible."

"Well, that's true," said Shirley.

Evelyn grinned and set the mug down. "I like watching those Saturday-night movies you turn off. I love seeing the good guys win."

"So we're agreed?" Anne asked.

"Yes," came from the other three.

"Should we tell Liam?"

"I think we should," said Shirley. "I know it might worry him, but he needs to know. In the end I would love nothing more than to find out it's that seriously cute EMT who's asked Katie out a couple of times."

"Stalker EMT? Sounds wonderful." Evelyn's dry tone said it didn't sound wonderful at all.

Shirley laughed. "I don't think he's a stalker. He's just interested, but she's not, so that gets a little dicey. He's persistent."

"What's his name?"

"Drew Mason. Andrew Mason. With CCEMS. He's on the tactical team as needed. Otherwise he's down here."

"Down here" meant the lower end of the peninsula—the historic district and tourist-trap areas.

Years back Charleston County had formed their own EMS department after using competitive ambulance services. Turned out competition for patients wasn't the best way to run an emergency medical response team. With specialized tactical, motor, water, and bike units, trained CCEMS professionals were often mere minutes from a call, and that vicinity sometimes meant the difference between life and death.

"Shall we all meet to talk with Seamus tomorrow morning?" asked Anne.

"I can't," said Joy. "I have an appointment with a local merchandiser who specializes in handcrafted items at reasonable prices. I'm not sure if her idea of 'reasonable' jives with mine, but we're getting together first thing tomorrow."

Evelyn raised her hand. "I'm in early tomorrow, so Anne and I can meet with Seamus as early as he can fit us in. But what about Garrison?" she asked. "He's not going to like being left out of the loop."

"You're right, of course," said Anne. "And none of us wants to get fired for leaving the administration out of the loop. But getting the two of them together won't be easy. Can we have Seamus fill Garrison in?"

"That sounds good," said Shirley. "It limits people that know to a minimum initially but spreads out the responsibility of keeping Katie safe." She paused before continuing. "I want to mention that there's something messed up about this timing. To the best of my knowledge, Katie has only recently sent off her DNA sample."

The other three women nodded.

"So how could anyone connected with Atlanta and the adoption be aware of it? And yet that's where the inquiry took place, according to Liam. Someone was asking questions there. But that couldn't be related to the DNA test, because the results aren't out yet."

"So who's targeting her now?" Joy posed the question Anne was thinking. "And...why?"

Chapter Five

"Someone's stalking Katie?" Seamus's brows shot up when Anne and Evelyn met with him the following morning. "Please tell me you're kidding, because I'm only on my second cup of coffee, ladies, and the last thing I want to hear is that someone's stalking anyone. And I'm also wondering why she hasn't said anything to me."

Anne and Evelyn exchanged looks. "It's an odd situation, Seamus."

Seamus offered them a deadpan expression. "When isn't it? Have a seat. Please. Tell me what's going on." He pulled out the flip notebook he carried in his back pocket and grabbed a pen.

Anne reiterated what Liam had told them, and Evelyn explained Katie's concerns. "Maybe she didn't want to worry you," said Anne. "I know she felt weird about the whole thing, as if she was making something out of nothing."

"Except it's not nothing if it's worrying her," said Seamus. "Katie doesn't overreact. That's part of what makes her so good at her job here." He frowned. "I'll talk to Garrison. And I'd like to talk to her grandfather too."

"I can pass that message along," said Anne, but Seamus shook his head.

"I'll do that later myself. I want to hear what's going on straight from her. And I'll fill Garrison in. He needs to know there's a potential situation. You said there was an irate patient that could be involved?"

Anne nodded. "Lee Spencer. Her husband passed away in October in the ER when Katie was on duty."

He wrote something then closed his notebook. "All right then." He stood.

That was their cue. The women stood too. "Thank you, Seamus." Anne put a hand on his arm. He always wore a sport coat but rarely a tie, giving him that semicasual TV-hero appearance. Rumpled enough to be tough, suited-up enough to be professional. Seamus was a man who could pull that look off.

"I want you all to be careful." He aimed a serious look at them. "I don't know how you keep ending up in the middle of things, but I don't want anyone hurt. My uncle retired from the Atlanta force three years back. I know they have their problems, so I understand Detective Holden's hesitancy. All it takes is a couple of bad apples and things go downhill mighty quick. This won't go any further unless we encounter a situation where it must. Then you've got to trust my judgment."

"We will." Anne patted his arm. "We know you'll keep it low-key but thorough. That's all we can ask."

On the way down the hall toward Records, the sounds of renovation reverberated not-so-softly from a room to their right, a room in the throes of becoming an internal Mercy Hospital museum. The noise, deliberately slated for pre-busy hospital hours, made Evelyn smile. "The sound of those nail guns is music to my ears," she told Anne.

"I love seeing this dream of yours come true," Anne replied. "Just the thought of having a room filled with the hospital's history and all the good it has done makes me glad. And you never gave up, Evelyn."

For years Evelyn had wanted, encouraged, and worked toward a spot that would showcase Mercy Hospital's rich history and heritage in their beloved city. With a recent round of approvals, her dream was about to become a reality.

"I always believed it would happen eventually," Evelyn said. "I couldn't let it go, even when the hospital took financial hits, because this place has seen so much and come so far, and that should be recognized."

"Amazing," Anne agreed. "I'd love to help arrange displays when you're ready. Call on me anytime, okay?"

"I would appreciate extra hands. Thank you!" Evelyn hurried off into Records just as Anne's pager jangled a summons to the lobby. Aurora Kingston was running the desk today, and when Aurora was on, pagers pinged continuously, as if hitting the volunteers' numbers gave her a feeling of power.

Anne hurried that way. "I'm here," she said brightly.

Aurora threw her hands up. "I'm so glad. I was dreadfully afraid you'd be out after yesterday morning's frightening incident, and I wouldn't have blamed you, Anne."

"And yet here I am," replied Anne cheerfully. It did no good to try to talk Aurora down. She ran on all eight cylinders, and Anne had discovered a long time ago that it was better to just smile and nod. Which is what she did now.

"The ER needs help restocking supplies, but I need you in patient discharge from nine o'clock on. All right?"

"Sounds good." Anne stowed her bag beneath the counter and headed to the emergency room.

It wasn't a room, of course. It was a center, done in a medically friendly style with cubicles surrounding a centralized nursing station. Trauma was off to one side, separated by swinging doors, and a pediatric unit flanked the other side. That bit of geographical distance kept impressionable kids from the sights and sounds of the day-to-day ER.

As she neared the access door, Seamus approached from the hall linking the ER to the surgical elevators. Between them was Katie, head down, typing on an electronic notebook. She glanced up and spotted Anne. She started to smile, but then she must have caught sight of Seamus.

She paused, and appreciation widened her eyes.

She reached to tuck her hair behind her ear, a move Anne remembered quite well.

Seamus moved alongside the curved station. "Can we talk sometime today? Before you leave this afternoon?"

Katie lowered her tablet. "That depends. Does this invite include anything from Ginger's bakery?"

"Probably not today because my day just got busier, but I will happily prioritize that for tomorrow. When are you free?"

She made a face as the sounds of incoming patients came through from the busy waiting area. "When I clock out at three."

"Then three it is." Seamus smiled. He leaned an elbow against the counter separating them and just stood there for a few long and interesting seconds.

Katie held his gaze as if she couldn't or wouldn't break the connection. Then she noticed Anne, leaned back, and folded her arms. "You told."

"Just Seamus, because he's privy to a gazillion camera angles," Anne replied. "We only have four sets of eyes, and those are busy working throughout the day. We want you safe, Katie."

"I know." She tipped her gaze back up to Seamus's. "There is most likely nothing going on, and I'm probably borrowing trouble."

"Except you don't do that, Katie," said Seamus in his firm but gentle voice.

"No."

His face softened. "Then let's combine forces. Stop down at my office before you head home, okay? And I promise to drop by Ginger and Bud's place tomorrow. First thing."

She smiled. "In that case, yes. I'll be there. And Seamus?"

He lifted one brow her way.

"Thank you."

He gave her a look as if there was nothing to thank him for. "No problem. See you later." He walked away, and when he disappeared at the turn just past the surgical elevators, Katie brought her attention back to Anne. She sighed.

"We had to clue him in."

"I know." Katie grimaced. "It's not that I'm upset about him knowing, it's that I'm upset that something like this is happening. It's unnerving. I'm getting paranoid, thinking someone is watching me. Waiting for me. Lurking."

A shiver tracked its way down Anne's spine. "Has anything else happened?"

"No. But I expect it to, and that's the anxious part. And I'm not an anxious person."

"I know." Katie had been working at Mercy for a while. They'd gotten to know each other because Anne's duties took her to all corners of the hospital, including the ER when folks were transferred upstairs for admission. Or when people needed to be wheeled out.

"Seamus is a good guy. He's easy to talk to."

"He is," admitted Katie. "He's going to wonder why I didn't just bring it to him first."

"And that's when you remind him that you didn't want to make a big deal out of something that might be nothing." Shirley had come alongside in time to hear the end of the conversation. "We have incoming, Katie."

"Did you know Seamus's mom delivers homemade cookies for the security teams?" asked Anne.

Katie looped her stethoscope around her neck. "He said she's self-conscious about going straight back to his office, so she leaves them at the front desk."

"And always includes a plate for us," Anne told her. "She's got a thoughtful heart. And a good son."

"You understand why we had to tell him, don't you?" Shirley aimed a more serious look at Katie. "We couldn't hide something that might hurt you or put others at risk."

"I should have done it myself." Katie tapped a finger on the electronic notebook. "A part of me figured if I ignored it, it would go away, but I know that's foolish. And I'm not generally foolish."

"Been there, done that," Shirley told her.

"You fill Seamus in on what's going on, and we'll keep eyes and ears open," Anne promised as Katie crossed the station toward the new patients. "For now, I'm supposed to be restocking things over here. Shirley, can you tell me what needs to be done?"

"Definitely." She led the way to the far side of the ER where storage closets and delivery carts lined the hall. When they got there, she lowered her voice. "Your meeting with Seamus went okay?"

"Yes. He's going to bring Garrison in on it. Other than that, he'll keep things quiet. But he's concerned."

"Aren't we all? I keep hoping Liam's wrong, but I can't deny there's a lump in my throat when I think about it. Liam Holden was one of those cops that always got it done and got it done right. Years back another investigator told me 'He's got gut.' That means he senses the right and wrong of a situation."

"If we go riling up an Atlanta mob, I won't have to worry about racketeers killing me. Ralph will beat them to it," whispered Anne. "But who's going to suspect a bunch of middle-aged-and-up women of anything? We're pretty innocuous."

"Nothing wrong with that," Shirley declared. "You know where things go here?"

Anne winked. "Not my first rodeo." Shirley went back to patient care while Anne restocked the shelves of the supply closets then wheeled the tall transport carts down to the silver elevators. She returned all three to the basement level. When she moved back toward the elevators, the doors had just quietly closed and the Up arrow flicked past the first floor.

Patients would be discharged soon, and she couldn't wait for a poky elevator, so she took the stairs.

She came up around the corner toward the second-floor entry door and surprised a woman standing there. "Do you need directions?" asked Anne. It wasn't hard to get lost in the busy labyrinth that had become Mercy Hospital with its numerous extensions, new wings, professional buildings, and parking areas. "I'm one of the hospital volunteers."

"I don't call this excuse for a facility a hospital," snapped the woman. "I know exactly where I am, thank you. I'm right where I was when some sorry excuse for a doctor came and told me my husband was gone. Just like that. No warning. No kindness. No expectation. Gone within minutes of me getting a phone call saying he was coming to the hospital and then—" Tears began running down her cheeks. "And then—"

"I know the 'and then,'" Anne began, but the woman cut her off quickly.

"You're a widow?"

Anne shook her head. "No, but my husband's a pastor and we've sat with a lot of—"

The woman's cheeks tightened. Her eyes narrowed. She leaned in, as if threatening. The maneuver worked, and Anne wanted to take a step back. "Sitting with grief isn't the same as having it drive an arrow straight into your heart, especially when it didn't have to happen." The woman's voice shook with anger or grief. Maybe both. "I hate when people offer pretend commiseration. If you've never lost your beloved spouse, you have no idea what I'm going through. None!"

Anne knew loss.

She knew the fight for her daughter's life, a precious child taken by the rigors of leukemia over three decades ago. She knew the hopelessness of watching Ariane slip away and the helplessness of her hands, but the woman didn't stay to hear Anne's words.

She whirled about and pounded down the stairs, making her steps as loud and obnoxious as she could.

Anne's heart rate had accelerated when the woman first began talking and hadn't slowed down much since. The pounding footsteps only accentuated the emotion. She took a deep breath, then slipped through the access door and found Shirley. "What does Lee Spencer look like?"

"Tall-ish. Thin. Brown hair. Lighter eyes, but not blue. Hazel, maybe? Angry. Really, really angry. Why?"

"I think I just ran into her. There." She pointed toward the back of the ER that led to the silver elevators. "She was standing on the landing, staring at the door," she whispered. "I asked if she needed directions, and she snapped and told me she knew exactly where she was. Right where she'd been when they told her that her husband died."

"She was actually just inside the door, but she's been advised to stay out of the hospital after some verbal threats." Distress drew Shirley's brows together. "Do you think she could be angry enough to be Katie's stalker?"

Anne didn't know. "Hiding in the stairwell isn't exactly obvious except to us, maybe. Visitors and patients rarely use the stairs—they wait for the elevator. But maybe…" Anne hated to even suggest this, but there was little choice. "Maybe she was waiting there, hoping Katie would use that door."

"I've got shivers." Shirley frowned.

"Me too, but I need to get up to four. They've got discharges ready."

"We'll talk later."

"And fill Seamus in."

Shirley gave her a grim look and a thumbs-up.

The rest of the morning passed quickly, but Anne couldn't get the confrontation out of her mind. At midday she texted Ralph. He was volunteering as an on-site chaplain, a new calling for him now that he'd retired as the pastor of St. Michael's Church just a few blocks away. CAN I SEE YOU?

CAN'T THINK OF ANYTHING BETTER, he texted back.

ANGEL STATUE 12:45.

SEE YOU THEN.

The Angel of Mercy statue had withstood scores of perils in its nearly two hundred years standing sentinel outside the hospital. The statue and the adjacent wing weren't destroyed by the destructive fires of the Civil War. The rest of the hospital had fallen, but the Angel Wing had survived the onslaught. Locals attributed that to the blessings of the angel, a sign of hope in a time of trouble. The statue and the beautifully maintained gardens around it still offered respite and inspiration. No matter what the weather—hurricanes and tornadoes, excepted, of course—people would pause and pray. A big busy hospital housed lots of folks in need of prayer. The Angel of Mercy was the perfect reminder that God lives and loves. Even in the darkest hours.

Anne met Ralph there shortly before one. She gave him a quick hug that felt marvelous but then launched into her story. "I've only got a few minutes," she told him. "It seems like pediatrics is trying to clear out all the beds they have in a two-hour period, but that's probably because they wanted to get elective surgeries done during the school break. I ran into a woman this morning," she explained. She glanced around to make certain no one could hear her. "She lost her husband last fall."

His brows drew down in sympathy. "I'm sorry to hear that."

Anne squeezed his hands. He was such a dear, kind man. He could never find his glasses on top of his head or the current book he was reading or even his shoes at times, because when his thoughts shifted to God and faith or the human condition, he lost track of everything else. Anne was pretty sure that was why God had sent him an organized wife.

"She's angry." She settled on one of the benches, and Ralph sat down beside her. "Furious. And not with God. With us. With Mercy. I found her lurking in the stairwell this morning, and I'm afraid she might mean someone harm. She unnerved me, and not too much upsets me."

"I have wished things would unnerve you a little more than they do at times," said Ralph, "so the fact that she did is telling. Did she threaten anyone?"

"Not today. But her voice, her posture, and her anger are threatening. She yelled at me," Anne said. She didn't like to admit it, but she had a thing about being yelled at. No one got to do it. Ever. She wasn't a yeller, and she expected similar treatment in return.

"Oh, that pushed your buttons," said Ralph, and he almost smiled. "I learned my lesson about that a long, long time ago."

"Yelling is unseemly and unnecessary," said Anne. "I *know* that I'm sensitive to it, but it still galled me that she did it. Once I was upstairs working, I kept wondering what I could have done to make the situation better, and I couldn't think of a thing. I was disappointed, because she's obviously grief-stricken."

"Or guilt-ridden."

Anne met his gaze.

"You and I both know how powerful grief can be," he said. "But grief compounded by guilt is even worse, because once the person is gone, it's too late to fix the guilt part. Maybe what you're dealing with isn't just her grief, but grief and guilt. She might not be able to discern between the two. Occasionally, those folks sometimes border on mental instability."

"You mean they're dangerous."

He grimaced. "Sometimes. Not often, but irrational thought in a grieving mind can become a catalyst. What I'm saying is there might not be anything you or anyone can do. We pray and we let God do what God's best at doing—fixing things."

"I kind of didn't want to fix her."

"No?"

Anne sighed. "I just went on with my day. Stewing. And wishing I were a better person."

He laughed. "Impossible, Anne. The Lord hasn't made a better person, and I'm blessed every day to call you mine." He gave her another hug. "Can we go out for supper tonight? I feel like eating by the water before it gets too warm. What do you think?" He leaned back and looked down at her. "A couple of oldie but goodies on a date?"

"I'd love it. Can we eschew fancy, though?"

"Will you promise to stop using words like *eschew*? Because that's ridiculous."

"Agreed. For now. I do like nice words, Ralph."

He stood and pulled her up with him. "I know. And you're the best partner for a guy who likes crossword puzzles. Doubly so because you don't have the patience to do them yourself."

"I'd rather peel hot red peppers with my bare hands," she replied cheerfully. "Maybe that's why we've had a great marriage, Ralphie."

He rolled his eyes like he always did when she used the name Ralphie.

"Whatever works, Annie." He leaned down and gave her a quick kiss. "I'm grabbing coffee from Joy and heading back to the stroke unit. Love you."

"I love you too."

They returned inside together before splitting directions. Anne hurried to discharge with a gentler heart and a clearer mind.

Her run-in had drummed up a lot of mixed feelings, and although she'd wondered about having Ralph around her volunteer site after he'd retired, it had turned out much better than she'd expected.

And today she got a date out of the deal, so that was better yet.

Chapter Six

Charleston, South Carolina
1967

Regina Bashore took the bus to work most nights, but if Charles was done at the barbershop, he'd take her down to Mercy Hospital and drop her off.

Regina was smart, well-spoken, and skilled, and when she'd applied for a job at Mercy, the Director of Nursing agreed. She'd hired her over two years back and put her in the Special Care Nursery, exactly where she wanted to be.

She walked in and went straight up to the third floor. She hummed as she went, smiling and nodding to this one and that. Some days it was easy to smile.

Some days it wasn't.

On those days she'd stop by that pretty statue outside and sit a minute with the angel, say her prayer to God, and be on her way.

She scrubbed up, then used her hip to push open the nursery's swinging doors. "Hey, Tricia. Martie. How we all doing tonight?"

Two rows of Isolettes, one on either side of the room, lined the outer walls of Mercy's Special Care Nursery. Two tables with special warming trays took up the center, and several rocking chairs, recent additions, sat empty.

"All is well at the moment," Martie told her. "But we've got a primigravida in labor about four weeks early."

"We'll ask the Good Lord to bless this new arrival with strong lungs and a healthy size," Regina said. A solid gestational weight and suitably developed lungs made a huge difference for these born-early infants.

Mary Louden came in then. She and Regina shared the night shift this week. She smiled at Regina but didn't interrupt as Martie went down the list of babies. Only eight right now, and none in serious straits. Warmth, food, and nurturing were the mainstays for most of these wee ones, and the Special Care Nursery staff was trained in all aspects of neonatal care. These babies needed that extra dose of patience, warmth, touch, and attention, and almost every nurse in this department took time to do it.

Less than two hours later the OB staff trundled in their new occupant.

Small, just under five pounds. The doctor tucked her Isolette onto Regina's side and barked the stats but not in a mean manner. He used a let's-get-this-done no-nonsense tone that Regina respected. Then he faced her. "Mother is frantic, blood loss, and the father is with her. I've assured her we've got the best of the best in our nursery." He exchanged a look with her and Mary. "Because I know that's true."

It was great praise, but Regina knew their limitations. Even with mechanical incubators that helped so many infants survive, the problems of preemies filled a wide spectrum with few answers.

But she had faith, and the whole Special Care Nursery team prayed over these babies, and prayed often.

Regina tended the new arrival.

Apgar Score: 6 at birth. 8 at five minutes. That was good, but her color was pale for a wailing newborn.

She paged the on-call pediatrician and filled him in.

He wasn't up the hall in the regular nursery. He was on the pediatric ward, one resident, overseeing both baby nurseries and the entire floor for nearly ten hours. And tired, by the look of him. "Whatcha got, Regina?"

"Not enough color, Doctor." She led him to Baby Stanton's incubator. "Decent Apgar, not overly small, but she's not as pink as I'd like."

The resident checked the newborn over with firm but gentle hands. He had a good touch, and when he frowned, Regina's heart clenched. "She's got a heart problem."

Regina had suspected as much.

"Can't say how bad and what can be done. You know there's experiments going on with heart surgeries, but we don't have anything for a baby this small."

"Then we pray," Regina said. "We storm the heavens and ask God to watch over her. You need to go see her mama, Doctor. She and this child's daddy need to know what's happening. And if she wants to come down here and sit with this little one, you have them wheel her on down. I can't imagine being away from my child if she was in distress."

The doctor hesitated. "They don't get mothers up that quickly, Regina. In general."

"We're not talking in general, we're talking in particular," Regina said. "If this baby makes it, all well and good, but if she doesn't, then we need to give her mama and daddy time with her."

"Both of them?" The young doctor's eyebrows shot up over his mask.

"Are you a father yet?"

He winced. She knew he was, and what daddy wouldn't want to be with his baby child? "I'll take care of it."

"And Mary and I will set up a spot." They had a curtained area at the far end of the room. In training, Regina had encountered sorrowful parents who never got to see or hold their little ones as they went home to God, but Regina's mama had talked about delivering babies back in the Second World War and how it blessed those mamas to have time with their babies, no matter how much time it was.

She and Mary rearranged the Isolettes so that the Stanton baby was in the corner. Rockers flanked the incubator. Mary grimaced when she spotted one of the OB nurses pushing a woman down the hall. The young father followed. He looked scared and totally out of his element.

Regina met them at the door. "You have to scrub up," she told them. "Good and long, hands, nails, and a face washing isn't a bad thing, either. And then you put on those cotton gowns and the masks and gloves."

The young man seemed taken aback. "We do all that to see our baby?"

"There are nine babies in here, and we don't want to be spreading germs to any of them, and you are going to look so good in that blue cotton!" She kept it light, and it almost worked, but his mouth turned down again.

Fear and determination fought for his wife's expression. Determination won. "We'll do whatever we need to, Nurse."

"Regina," she told the young mother.

"I'll show them how to scrub up, Regina." The OB nurse motioned back to the nursery. "I know you're needed in there."

She was. She returned, rescrubbed, and put on fresh gloves and a new mask.

The department had recently put the rockers in place because someone donated them after reading a study about preemies needing less isolation and more time with people. More contact. They hadn't been used much yet, but when the young couple was scrubbed and gowned, Regina showed them to the corner. "Here we are." She spoke softly. "You can't be picking her up. Not yet. But if you slip your hands in here"—she indicated the portals—"and talk to her and sing to her, that might be the very medicine she needs."

"Talkin' isn't going to fix her heart, Nurse." The young man stared at her as if she had two heads.

"God and Mother Nature are on that task," she replied firmly. "Some babies' hearts grow stronger. Some do not. But whatever happens with Baby Stanton's heart—"

"Jeannine," breathed the young mother, and she offered her baby a look of such love that Regina's heart clenched. "Jeannine Mary Stanton."

"A beautiful name." Regina looked at the young mother.

The mother stared back, and at that moment Regina felt a connection of love and faith and strength between them. "Then maybe I should pick another," whispered the mother. "Because our daughter might need a warrior's name to get through this."

"She's got that for the middle, because I don't know a stronger woman than the Good Lord's own mama," said Regina firmly. "It's a fine name, Mrs. Stanton."

"Susie."

"And I'm Hollis."

Regina shared a small smile with them.

They didn't know she was breaking protocol. They didn't know she might be putting her job on the line to give them time with their baby girl because fathers hadn't been allowed into the Special Care Nursery before. All they knew was that they had time with their ailing child, and for Regina Bashore, that was enough.

Chapter Seven

Anne sent a group text to her friends and Liam when things slowed down shortly after two. Tomorrow morning early coffee?

A combination of thumbs-ups and checkmarks came back to her, and after a lovely, calm evening by the harbor with Ralph, she was ready to face whatever the next day might bring.

She parked her car in the spot near the hospital an old friend had given them as a pastoral retirement gift and hurried down the street toward the café. As she rounded a corner, the handle of her bag snagged the arm of one of the park benches. The weight of the bag and the solidity of the bench pulled her back sharply.

"Whoa." A man caught her arm before she fell backward onto the concrete. "Ma'am, are you all right?"

"I am because you grabbed hold," Anne said. She unsnagged her bag and shifted it to the other side. "My husband keeps telling me I pack too much into this thing, and a crash to the pavement would have proven him right. Thank you so much."

The man smiled. It was a nice smile. Friendly. "Just glad I was here to help."

"I am too. Thanks again."

He went one way. She hurried another, and she kept the bag tucked on her other side. Just in case.

Evelyn had retrieved the coffee order this morning, including one for Liam. They gathered between the hospital and the harbor. It always amazed Anne that this side of the Charleston peninsula overlooked the North Atlantic, an ocean that had seen storms, perils, and shipwrecks up and down the East Coast. No storms threatened today's peace. The water was calm and serene with a light breeze riffling the early leaves.

Anne filled the group in on her encounter with Lee Spencer. "I looked her up online before we went to supper last night." She handed each of them a printed picture. "This is what she looks like. Only angrier. Much, much angrier."

Liam seemed unconvinced.

"What are you thinking?" Shirley asked him.

He folded the printout and tucked it into a pocket. "Far too convenient."

"Sometimes that's the case," Joy replied.

"It is," he agreed. "But I don't think that's the case now."

"By what reasoning?" Trust Shirley to delve for a solid response, and Liam didn't disappoint.

"The background. I admit I'm conflicted because I know the history. That knowledge can give me tunnel vision. On top of that, Katie's my granddaughter. I'm understandably protective. Since I helped facilitate the adoption, I bear a different responsibility. I knew there was a possible threat lurking in the background, but I also knew that the records were kept confidential enough that no one could find Katie. Ever. The DNA thing is a major concern now. This wasn't something adoptive families had to worry about twenty-five years ago, but it's a current reality. So maybe I'm foreseeing problems where none currently exist, at least until that test comes back. Maybe this woman is the culprit and I'm grasping at straws, but my gut says otherwise."

Shirley had mentioned Liam's gut before. How he sensed things in a way others couldn't. Anne had read enough mysteries to realize that some folks had more of a gift in that area. She believed she was one of them, and she felt the same way Liam did. Lee Spencer could be the person of interest, but—

Liam added one more thought. "In general, I've found that people who are upfront about their anger are less likely to act on it, whereas the quiet ones find insidious ways to seek revenge or resolution."

"Normally I would concur," said Evelyn. "But I still want to check out Lee Spencer. I'd like to find out more about her."

"I'm free tonight," said Anne. "I'm not seeing Addie until Saturday, so I've got time. Ralph is meeting a couple of friends for golf."

"I need to be with Mama," said Shirley.

"If we meet at your place we solve that problem and get the pleasure of Regina's company," said Joy. "I've been wanting to compare notes with her about some history. I'll order supper. I remember your mama saying she's partial to jambalaya, and that's the special at Crabby Moe's today."

Shirley agreed instantly. "Mama would love all of you being over with or without food, but you know she loves good jambalaya. And knowing Mama, she'll whip up a dessert of some sort."

"Perfect." Joy's gentle smile punctuated the arrangement. "How's five thirty for everyone? Detective, would you like to join us?"

"Regretfully, no, but I appreciate being kept in the loop. Marion and I have a church council meeting."

"You're on the church council?" Shirley smiled at him. "How nice."

"Marion is," he corrected her. "She's a joiner. She's also a force to be reckoned with, which made her the perfect match for a guy who was married to his job as much as his wife. It cramps her style to have me underfoot all the time. She knows about all of this," he continued. "We don't keep things from one another, and she's worried. How do we explain to Sunny and Drake that we kept secrets about Katie's father twenty-five years ago?"

Shirley put a hand on his arm. "Liam."

He turned her way.

"You've been a man of honor for a long time. Your family knows that. They also know that your job has taught you to give out information on a need-to-know basis." She leaned in closer. "After nearly twenty years of ER duty, I've learned to do the same. I think your Sunny will understand that you didn't want shadows hanging over their daughter's head or their relationship. They didn't need to know back then." She paused and said, "But they do now. It won't be an easy conversation, but it's a necessary one."

He swallowed hard. "I've already set up a time with Sunny and Drake tomorrow afternoon. I don't know if they'll understand my holding back the organized crime connection, but for sure they would never understand being kept in the dark now. And then we tell Katie. She needs to be on her guard."

Anne sighed inside but kept her tone reassuring. "It's easier to slay a dragon on a level playing field. That way you can see him coming from all sides."

"I'll talk to you all afterward." Liam stood.

He headed to the harbor while they moved toward the hospital. As they drew closer to the door, Anne glanced back at Liam's departing figure.

A man had been sitting on one of the benches along the sidewalk. He'd had a newspaper up, reading, but as Liam took the turn toward the East Bay Café, the man folded the paper, tucked it beneath his arm, and stood. Then he went in the exact same direction.

Anne tried to make out his features, but the man's quick clip didn't allow close examination. Still, he looked like the man who'd saved her from the fall thirty minutes before, although she couldn't be sure from this distance. He was wearing similar pants and a light jacket, but that was essentially a uniform around these parts on April mornings, until shorts and sandals took their place.

"Anne. What's up?" Shirley had paused and turned back.

Anne pointed east, but the men had gone around a curve. "I think there might be someone following Liam." She pulled out her phone. She felt a little silly, but that wasn't about to stop her from texting him. MAN WITH TAN JACKET AND FADED JEANS BEHIND YOU. IS HE FOLLOWING YOU?

She waited a moment.

Her heartbeat revved up.

Impatience caused her to breathe quicker. And then Liam's text came back. NO ONE THERE.

She should feel relieved. She did, kind of. But not completely.

Joy, Evelyn, and Shirley were waiting. Joy was usually in the gift shop by now, not because she had to be, but because she liked getting things in order and changing things around. The extra time in the morning helped her feel ready to face the day.

"He says there's no one behind him."

"Good." The automatic doors slid open as Shirley moved forward. "I know Katie's working today, but she's off tomorrow. She's working the weekend, but I have this weekend off. And Joy is off too."

Joy nodded. "Eloise's soccer tournament. Two games Saturday and two on Sunday if storms don't delay things."

"And I'm helping paint the side rooms at Mother Emmanuel," noted Shirley.

"With Garrison." Anne grinned as she mentioned a fact that Shirley had conveniently left out.

"Parishioners working together for the common good," Shirley retorted, but she winked.

"And I'm at my niece's baby shower in Greenville," added Evelyn. "So who's around to keep an eye on things?"

As if on cue, Seamus McCord came whistling up the hallway of the angel wing. He spotted the women and paused. "Meeting of the Secret Sleuthing Society?" His light tone held a smile.

"Or a bunch of sweet, middle-aged women grabbing coffee to chat about the latest in mom jeans," replied Anne.

He laughed. "If only that were the case. What's up? I saw you exchange looks the minute you spotted me."

"We're all off this weekend, but Katie's working."

Nothing got by Seamus, it seemed. "Fortunately, I checked the schedule and saw that and took on those weekend shifts."

"They're giving you overtime?" Evelyn didn't have to pretend to be shocked, because overtime had been minimized except in dire need to keep finances in check for the remainder of the fiscal year.

"It seemed prudent," he said. "I had nothing going on, so being here isn't a hardship."

"And we know she'll be in good hands," noted Anne. "Thank you, Seamus."

"Glad to help. You coming this way?" he asked Evelyn.

She nodded. "Sure am." They went off toward their respective offices while Shirley, Anne, and Joy headed in the opposite direction. Shirley hurried down the back hall access to the ER, and Anne and Joy moved toward the bright and open front lobby.

Joy went left.

Anne went right. She stowed her bag, then checked the volunteer assignment sheet. Aurora had an app for volunteers, but Anne preferred laptops and printouts.

Vaccine clinic.

She wrinkled her nose as one of the other volunteers came by. "Anne, can you check and see where I'm at today? I'm behind. As usual." Pam Brown was one of those women who packed her days full and often felt rushed without ever seeming to be rushed. And always got everything done.

"You only feel behind, sugar." Anne smiled at her and pointed. "Discharge."

Pam frowned. "I'm never on discharge, because I tend to run wheelchairs into corners and walls and occasionally somewhat expensive planters. For some reason, admin frowns on that. So why today? Is the vaccine clinic closed?"

Anne shook her head. "No, they've got me there."

Pam's brows drew down tighter. "Aurora switched us? Without a reason or asking? That makes no sense. I don't mind discharge, but I'm a klutz, and we all know it."

"And you're experienced with the vaccine clinic. Would the clinic have requested a change?" Anne was as puzzled as Pam looked. Once in a while a new person would decide to change everything, including volunteers, but Pam shook her head.

"No. I've worked with this team for three years, and we've got a system. I say we switch."

"I agree. What's the worst they can do?" Anne smiled. "Cut our pay?"

"Exactly!" Pam laughed, handed Anne her bag, and hurried over to the clinic. Anne tucked the bag away and signed Pam's name into the roster. Then she went upstairs. By the time she got to the silver elevators, two discharge calls had come in.

She escorted the two patients down, then doubled back toward the far side of the ER to make sure the vaccine clinic hadn't wanted her for a specific reason. The walk-in clinic was tucked into a low-access corner beyond the ER. It was serviced by local nurses to get people in and out quickly. The expanded parking of the ER helped, but a lot of folks who came to Mercy for vaccines came by bus, and as she turned the corner, she realized why she'd been assigned to the clinic this morning.

Regina Bashore was walking in the far entrance. She spotted Anne and waved. "Anne! Hello! I'm so glad you're here!"

"Regina." Anne hurried forward. Regina was healthy, but memory issues had begun thwarting her lately. She was just about to hug Regina when Shirley popped her head around the corner from the ER.

"Mama, you made it just fine!"

"I've been taking the bus to these hospital doors for decades, Daughter." Regina rolled her eyes, then crinkled them in a smile. "I expect not too much has changed. I even told the driver where I needed a transfer, and he made sure I got off there. A lovely man, he was."

"Good." Shirley never belabored her mother's issues, but like the good nurse she was, she quietly removed barriers that would mess with Regina's success and her quality of life.

"I didn't know Anne would be here."

"And yet here I am," said Anne. "Let's get you checked in, all right?"

Shirley kissed her mother's cheek and went back to work. Regina had worked at Mercy for nearly forty years, so when Pam spotted the elderly woman, she shared a look of understanding with Anne and stood. "Anne, let me change with you for a bit. I could use a walk or two."

"Perfect." Anne took over the check-in process at the vaccine site for the next hour while Pam went upstairs for discharge and didn't run into too many corners.

Or so she said. And if she did, well... Hopefully she was going slow.

Chapter Eight

SHIRLEY TEXTED ANNE A QUARTER-HOUR later. LUNCH BY THE ANGEL WITH MAMA, 11:45?

Anne sent a thumbs-up back, and when she and Regina emerged into the bright sunny day, she blinked, and Regina slowed down.

They were approaching the angel statue. The midday sun reflected off the pavement, bright and bold. Regina paused. She peered. Then she frowned.

"Mama, what is it?" Shirley had chosen a nearby patio-style table. Katie had just packed up her sparkly little satchel and was turning their way.

Regina sighed, then smiled. "Just my aging brain and tricks of light. I saw this pretty young lady and my heart did one of those quick turns, because she reminded me of an old friend. And my old friend's daughter, more like it. We used to meet here at the statue whenever she was in town. Oh, the times Susie and I had together, talking babies, praying over babies, praying for so many things."

"Did she work here?" asked Katie, and Regina shook her head.

"No." The memory softened Regina's expression as she shared the past with the three other women. "I took care of her baby in the early days of the Special Care Nursery, long before it became a

NICU. She and that sweet baby touched my heart and my soul, one of those Holy Spirit moments when someone waltzes into your life and you just know they're supposed to be there."

"I love those times," said Katie. She reached out a hand. "You're Shirley's mother, aren't you?"

"Regina Bashore, former RN right here at Mercy and freshly vaccinated against all manner of things an old woman needs to guard against."

"Katie McNamara. I have the pleasure of working with your daughter."

"She's a wonderful woman and a fine nurse," declared Regina. Then she paused again, still studying Katie. "I don't mean to be staring hard, it's just something about you reminds me of Susie. A nicer woman you'd never meet, so kind and good, although her choice in husbands wasn't the best."

"I've seen that happen a time or two," said Katie.

"But she and that sweet baby of hers, we were such good friends. The best of friends. We were sisters in Christ, praying and getting little Jeannine back to health, talking to the sweet Lord right here at this lovely statue long before the hospital was a maze of this, that, and the other thing. Simple women for a simpler time."

"And you passed your love of helping folks on to me." Shirley had brought lunch for both of them. She laid it out on the table as she spoke. "For which I am ever grateful, Mama."

"A servant's heart." Regina smiled at Shirley, Anne, and Katie. "It got passed on to Shirley, for certain. My oldest is more a business-as-usual kind of gal, but Shirley would have gotten on well with Susie and Jeannine because they had servants' hearts too."

"Have you ever heard from Jeannine's husband?" asked Shirley. "I haven't thought about Jeannine in a long while. She passed away from a heart condition when I was a teenager, leaving Kevin a widower with two little girls," she explained to Anne and Katie. "It was a dreadful heartache for him, I'm sure. I know it broke Mama's heart to lose Jeannine and then never see her husband or the girls again." She added that last with a look of sympathy to Regina.

"I'm so sorry." Katie's expression changed to reflect Shirley's.

Regina's eyes filled.

She took a breath, then grasped the back of a chair. Anne knew it wasn't to steady herself from falling. She was guarding against an onslaught of unexpected emotion. She and Shirley moved to flank the kindly woman, because waves of emotion were sometimes as difficult as loss of memory. "I've not heard a word in all these years. I expect he wanted to start anew with those two dear girls, and who can blame him?" Regina sighed. "I promised their grandma I'd see to her girl, and it felt odd being cut off after making a promise like that, but life holds twists and turns, doesn't it?"

"It does." Katie slung her bag over her arm. "Ladies, I'm due back inside, but enjoy your lunch. This is my favorite spot," she told Regina and Anne. "I gravitate here, to the statue, whenever I can break away. It called to me even before I was hired here, back when I was doing clinicals. It's a place of peace. Almost a place of protection, if you know what I mean."

"I know exactly what you mean," declared Regina. "And I feel the same way. Like I'm drawn."

"Yes." Katie's quick smile could light up a room. "Just so. See you inside, Shirley."

"Yes, ma'am."

They sat down. Shirley blessed the Lord and the food, but before she could eat, Regina touched her arm. "Doesn't Katie remind you of Jeannine, Shirley?"

"Well, she has blond hair and blue eyes, Mama. But other than that? Not really. Or maybe," she amended with a shrug. "Her voice, maybe. More than her looks."

"The voice. The lilt. More like that, yes."

"A Southern drawl with a lilt of Irish laughter," offered Anne, and Regina laughed.

"That was Susie and Jeannine through and through. They made it through some troubled times up in Georgia, and Susie's husband was not exactly fond of our friendship," she went on. "He didn't like anything that took Susie's time and attention away from him. But Susie wouldn't cave. It wasn't her way to dismiss anyone, especially her friends. 'Not how I was raised, thank you very much,' she'd say to him. She used to say, 'Regina, Miss Molly taught me to make my life an alleluia, and that's exactly what I've done. Best I can, anyhoo.'"

"I forgot that about her," said Shirley. "And it's a perfect saying. For her and Jeannine."

Sadness claimed Regina's features. "I let her down."

Tears trickled from her eyes.

The rocking emotions were another sign of the brain's struggle, but this time seemed different to Anne. Less random. She put an arm around Regina from one side while Shirley did the same from the other.

"You did no such thing," said Shirley. "Mama, you did your best when you could, and things happen. God-things. Timing things.

You know you raised me up to believe that God's ways and His timing will get us through. I believe that was the case with Susie and Jeannine. With Kevin and the girls. I don't blame him for wanting to start over, and I expect he's married to some wonderful woman, and she raised Emily and Amelia to be marvelous young women." She gave Regina a light squeeze. "I love you, Mama, and I love that good and blessed heart of yours. It makes me want to be a better person. Now all this emotional stuff is fine, but I'm on a schedule, and you know Dr. Barnhardt will not like me bein' late, nor will he appreciate me eating on the job. And this PB&J with your homemade cherry jam is the best yet. My compliments to the cook."

Regina blushed slightly.

The jam and Shirley's schedule drew her mind away from troubled times, but Anne heard the longing in her voice when she talked of years past…and it only made her hate Alzheimer's and all its related ailments a little more.

She walked Regina to the bus stop when lunch was over. She was going to clock back in once Regina was safely on her way home, but she took a minute to go back to the Angel of Mercy.

She'd prayed to God here many times. For Ariane. For Lili. For her sweet husband, for parishioners, for Addie, for patients. So many patients! She and the angel had a strong history, but hearing Regina talk about her old friend and the statue had touched her heart.

In a big, bustling city like Charleston, how many folks had stood or sat near this statue, heads bowed or hands folded? Or those who pretended not to pray while praying because they worried what others might think?

The Lord loves the sound of a choir...but first He hears the cries in the dark.

The sense of that saying struck a chord with her. She loved choir music. And she listened to praise and worship music on WAY FM, 100.9. But she understood a father's prayer and a mother's cry for help and knew the Lord heard those pleas even when His answer wasn't as hoped.

She wound her way back to the discharge loop at the far side of the hospital. As she approached the walk, she spotted Liam.

He wasn't alone.

A woman was addressing him. Her stance and posture added aggression to her words.

Normally Anne would have given them room to finish their discussion, but the current situation spurred her to Liam's aid. She marched forward and drew up alongside Liam. "Liam, so nice to see you here. Did you come to see me?"

Liam had been a detective a long time. He grabbed the opening she gave him. "I figured I'd make a surprise visit."

"And so you did." Anne smiled at him, then faced the woman. "I'm Anne Mabry. I help out here at the hospital."

"I don't care who you are." The fortysomething woman glared at Anne then Liam again as she bit the words out with intensity. "I came here because my mother's having heart surgery, and the last person I expected to see was one of the most dishonest, disreputable members of the Atlanta Police. And yet here he is, as if he's waiting for me. As if he hasn't already done enough to ruin our family."

Liam said nothing. He stood there, stoic, letting her vent.

"I knew you were in town." The woman lowered her voice. Not a whisper. A warning. "I've kept my eye on you and yours all these years."

A chill spiked its way up Anne's spine.

"My sainted mother moved us down here to get away from the press. The trials. The notoriety. We gave up everything to get away from the chaos you helped rile up, and I will never forgive you for ruining our family, Liam Holden. Winchesters don't forgive." She stuck her face closer to his. "And they never forget."

She pivoted and headed toward the ER entrance. She moved too quickly, though, and banged her shoulder into one of the doors. Anne was sure that added insult to injury, but she directed her attention to Liam. "That was rough."

He scrubbed a hand to the back of his neck and shrugged. "I helped put her father away for a very long time. The family accused me and the police force of planting evidence. A lot of fallout. A lot of folks hurt. It would have been awful for the Winchester kids to be in a local school up there. Their mom uprooted everything, moved them away, and changed their last name before the trial even began."

"She blames you."

"She blames everyone but her father. You heard her." He shrugged. "She believes he was set up."

"Was he?"

Liam rolled his eyes. "No. He was the setup guy. A kingpin. An embezzler. A racketeer. He redirected funds from a money-laundering enterprise that sent money offshore while leading one of the nastiest drug-running groups in Georgia. He got rich off of people's tragedies, and he deserved everything he got. But to his family he was a businessman who went to church on Sunday, played with babies, and kept his family out of harm's way."

"A double life."

"To the max. And he did it well. If you ever ran into Brock Winchester at a social gathering, you'd see a dedicated dad, determined to play ball with his kids and flip burgers on a summer Sunday."

"But there was another side to him."

He grimaced. "There was. But that's all Gwyneth and her brothers saw. I didn't realize she lives here in Charleston now. It wouldn't have changed my retirement plans, because Sunny and Drake are here, but I would have been better prepared mentally to see her if I'd known. Although I didn't recognize her. She was a child when it all went down. But she knew me the moment she saw me."

"That's hard to take from a job well done," noted Anne.

He shrugged. "Perils of the job. I sleep well. I did nothing wrong. I always felt bad for the innocents, Anne. The wives or husbands, the kids. Betrayal of trust is a horrible thing, and some kids have a really tough time with it. The family told the kids that their dad was framed by bad cops, and I was the lead detective on the case, so that makes me a target."

"And maybe put a target on Katie's back?" asked Anne.

He frowned. "No, I—" He paused. Looked toward the hospital. Then Anne. "She did say she's been keeping an eye on me for years."

"And it's an easy hop, skip, and jump from you to Katie with the internet. Was this the same case that put Katie up for adoption?"

"No, that was different. A mob enterprise. And that case was two years later."

"We need to add her to the list, Liam." Anne glanced at her watch and made a face. "I've got to get back inside, but text me Gwyneth's full name. She wasn't wearing a wedding ring, but she had a tan line as if she'd been wearing one recently."

"That's a good catch."

Anne shrugged and backed toward the building. "Does Katie know you're here?"

"I'm going to pop in and drop off taffy for the ER crew." He raised a familiar bag.

"Charleston's Own?" Anne was a big fan of the local saltwater taffy. "I'll have to drop by the ER a little later," she teased.

"I've had a lot of shoreline taffy in my time, and this is the best there is," said Liam. "We're not far from Old St. Andrew's Church, so swinging around to the Charleston's Own store off Ashley River is easy. Although I know they have it at the historic gift shop too. Over on Meeting Street."

Anne smiled as the door slid open. "In case of emergency taffy need?"

"Little stores tend to have little hours, and I'm a grab-it-when-I-need-it kind of guy. I don't want Katie to think I'm checking up on her," he added after a pause. "She knows I play golf over in Mount Pleasant. That makes the hospital kind of on the way."

"I think that's lovely." Anne texted the front desk that she was back and headed for the discharge area. "The gals and I will check out Gwyneth once we have her new name."

He made a face.

"It might be nothing, but if we're willing to examine the possibility of a vast unknown, plotting from Atlanta"—she made an expansive gesture with her hands—"there's nothing wrong with checking out a concrete and available threat right here. Sometimes the answers *are* right in front of us."

"It's worth checking. And nothing I'd considered," he admitted. He hesitated before continuing. "She is very angry. Still."

She was. Anne gave him a quick wave as she hurried down the hall leading to the back of the ER.

With over thirty years of working with Ralph to pastor a flock, she knew the dangers and downfalls of grudge holding. She'd seen unresolved emotions destroy families and wreck careers. She'd watched anger ruin people's futures. She knew how insidiously destructive the buildup could be.

All thoughts of that were put on hold with a busy afternoon of discharges, and when one of the silver elevators broke down, Anne had to wheel folks from the red or white elevators down and around the loop of the surgical waiting room to get them to the discharge pickup area. And each time she did, Gwyneth Winchester's eyes watched until Anne disappeared from sight.

On her last discharge, the Winchester woman was gone. Anne didn't realize how uncomfortable those passes were until she was able to breathe deeply as she escorted her final patient to the back doors. Just as she did, Shirley sent her a frantic text. MAMA NEVER MADE IT HOME.

Anne's heart clutched tight. YOU'RE SURE?

Shirley's reply came back quickly. YES. CHECKED WITH NEIGHBORS. NO ONE'S THERE. PHONE IS GOING STRAIGHT TO VOICE MAIL.

I'LL DRIVE YOU HOME, Anne texted back once she'd helped the young man to his car. THEN YOU DON'T HAVE ANY DETOURS. Shirley carpooled with another hospital worker to save money and help the environment, but Anne knew that the other woman had a couple of errands to run today. Normally a stop here or there was no big deal, but with Regina missing, a delay would make Shirley frantic.

NOW?

MEET ME AT THE ER ENTRANCE.

Anne drove quickly, but when she got to the expressway access ramp, a pile-up slowed traffic to a crawl and it was too late to duck out and take the back roads.

"You praying?"

Shirley nodded. "In panic mode. Which is ridiculous because I gave up panic mode a long time ago. Maybe it's good I've never had children of my own if I get this worked up over a missing mama."

"It's totally understandable, and you'd be a great mother," Anne retorted. "You're like the ideal blend of caring, empathy, and common sense, and that last commodity is most important. I could have used a bigger dose of that when I was younger, for sure. Has Garrison ever been married?"

Shirley shook her head. "Single. Like me. And I'm not old but I'm not young either, and you know the term they use for women my age having their first babies?"

Anne did and it was rough. "Elderly primigravida."

"I shudder at the very words, which are, of course, a silly slap in the face and no doubt made up by a man," said Shirley stoutly. "They should be changed to reflect the new day and age. Science and medicine have done a great many marvelous things."

They pulled into the driveway behind Shirley's car. Anne thrust hers into park, and the two women raced up the steps, through the door, and into a really good-smelling house. "Mama? Are you home?"

Regina flapped an apron at them when they barged into the kitchen. "Great sakes of mercy, what is wrong with you two?" she demanded, eyes wide. "Racing in here like that, about to scare a body to death! Is everything all right? Are the others still coming for supper like you planned?"

Her sweet drawl was music to Anne's ears, but Shirley wasn't quite so calm. "Mama. I've called and called, and your phone went straight to voice mail, even though I checked when you left the hospital and it was on."

"You called?" Regina's phone was on the counter. She picked it up and frowned. "Never even gave it a look, so that *is* my fault. I don't get out so often lately," she continued in a matter-of-fact voice. "Since I did, I took the bus on up to the Citadel."

The Citadel Mall was farther out on the bus route. After living in this house for decades, Regina knew her way around not only this part of the city but the city as a whole. But memory problems made this less than normal times.

"It was the perfect opportunity to take care of a few errands and do a little shopping. Then I hopped back on the bus when I was done, since they've made it so convenient to get 'round places. And Daughter"—she turned the burner under the teakettle on high—"it's impolite to be yapping on a phone while shopping, so I turned it off. But I was able to get the proper pecans and roasted peanuts we like so well, and that's a praline upside-down cake you smell in the oven. I don't know anything nicer smelling than that."

"It smells amazing," admitted Anne.

Shirley said nothing.

Anne wasn't sure if she had nothing to say or nothing she dared to say. Either way, it was a deafening silence for about ten seconds, and then she breathed.

It wasn't an easy choice.

Anne realized that.

But when Shirley exhaled that breath, Anne knew she'd come to terms with a difficult situation again.

"Did you bring the milk, Shirley?"

"I forgot." Shirley tugged Anne's hand toward the door. "We'll go grab it at the corner store."

"It's nearly a dollar more there," chided Regina.

"I know, Mama. But he needs business too, so a dollar now and again isn't a bad thing."

"That's truth."

Shirley stayed quiet until they got to the sidewalk, and then she unloaded. "It took everything I have. Everything," she stressed, "not to scold my sweet mother for running errands and getting home on her own, a task she's done for over seventy years, and all because I was worried. Instead of rejoicing in her independence, I panicked. Considering our discussion in the car, Anne, I wonder now what kind of horrible mother I would be, even if God's grace allowed. A good mother cannot allow herself to panic. After, sure. But never during a crisis. And I almost yelled at her for not coming straight home."

"But you didn't."

"It was close. Real close." Shirley wasn't strolling casually down the street. She went straight into power walk mode, and Anne hurried to keep up. "And then I realized I should celebrate every lucid moment and not think that I'm in charge of the entire universe."

"It's a tightrope, Shirley."

"I'm discovering that," Shirley acknowledged. "But she's not a child. She's an accomplished woman with so much strength and valor to her credit that I need to back off. Let her be the adult she's always been and let things happen as they may."

"That's not an easy stance for a take-charge woman."

"Ain't that the truth?"

Anne smiled as they entered the store. It was small, with crowded shelving, the kind of store that had gone out of style decades before, but the scent of fresh coffee and bread put some shine on the scuffed-up look. "Who makes the bread?" she wondered out loud. "It smells marvelous."

"My daughter." An elderly man was perched on a stool behind the worn counter. He had a seventies-style cash register with the pop-open drawer, but there was a card-reader off to the side beneath a sign that read CASH ONLY UNLESS YOU DON'T HAVE IT, AND THEN YOU CAN USE THIS STUPID THING THAT COSTS US MONEY AND RAISES PRICES.

Anne grabbed a loaf of freshly baked sesame-seed encrusted bread and put a twenty-dollar bill on the counter as Shirley came up from the back cooler with a gallon of milk. "A gallon?" She looked at the milk in surprise. "You all drink that much milk?"

"Mama is making her famous rice pudding for the potluck lunch to feed the painters at church this weekend. A good rice pudding takes its share of milk. Four percent too."

"The good stuff."

Anne paid the bill, and when Shirley tried to hand her money, she shied away. "No, ma'am. Consider it my donation to the painting project. Ralph and I make an annual donation to the AMEC fund. I love what they're doing and that you and Garrison and Regina are helping."

"She'll be there serving and cleaning up like she's done for years. My mama has given an example worth following."

"And that's probably the best thing for her," said Anne. "A task that keeps her busy and socialized now that the weather is nice again. Familiarity with the place and the people. Now, about Liam and Katie." She glanced around and softened her voice more out of habit than anything else. "The plot thickened today when I came across an angry woman who said she's keeping tabs on Liam and his family. I'll wait and tell all when the others are here, but Shirley, this might be the break we're looking for."

"With Easter coming next week, I'd be all right with that," declared Shirley. "But either way, I want to do whatever it takes to make sure Katie is safe and sound. I don't know how I'll forgive myself if anything happens to that girl. Not like it's our fault, but there's this gut feeling I have. Deep down, like there's evil out there with Katie's name marked on a list, and I want to thwart that evil in the worst way. And then I figure I'm being overdramatic and maybe silly."

Anne said, "I feel it too."

Shirley stopped. Evelyn's car was approaching the house and as she parked, Shirley held Anne's gaze. "For real?"

"Yes. I don't get real crazy about things, but I feel that sense of struggle. I don't know how. I don't know why. But I feel it. So you're not alone. Of course we both might be overreacting."

"I can't deny that possibility." Shirley made a face. "I am a bit excitable lately."

"Or we could both be quietly in tune with whatever is going on," Anne said. "Either way, let's do what we can to keep her safe and get answers for Liam. I'd love to have the police on board, but if Liam doesn't trust this to public knowledge, I don't either. My current needs are taking precedence, however." She jutted her chin toward Evelyn's car. "Joy's brought food, and that eleven forty-five lunch was over six hours ago. I'm not a six-hours-between-meals kind of gal."

Shirley grinned. "Me neither."

Chapter Nine

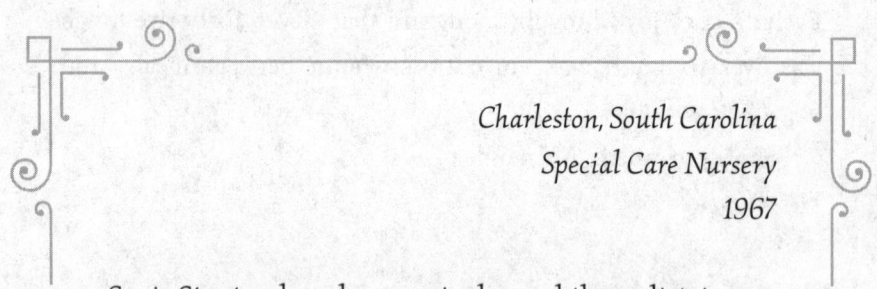

Charleston, South Carolina
Special Care Nursery
1967

Susie Stanton heard every single word the pediatric specialist told her, how there was a problem with Jeannine's heart. An unfixable problem.

She couldn't stay in the hospital to be near the baby. Insurance didn't cover having a baby, and the hospital costs were prohibitive, but she was grateful that Hollis's policy at the bank covered the baby's care. That was the most important thing of all.

Ellie had fussed, telling her to stay home and rest, but then Ellie's girls were born hale and hearty, so she'd never known this feeling. Susie was walking a ridgepole, teetering between hope and not daring to hope.

She hurried off the bus. There were a couple of aged buildings to her left and the hospital entrance to her right, but straight ahead was a kind of grotto. It was a misty morning.

Not raining misty—sea misty. The cool breeze off the harbor brought the mist inland, but even through the morning shadows and the mist, she saw the statue.

An angel statue.

She couldn't see it clearly from the curb, but there was no mistaking the shape, the wings, the form. When she drew closer, she realized the stone angel had her hands brought together in prayer. Just like Susie's had been for forty-eight hours.

"Susie?"

She turned as Regina hurried her way. "Regina. You're just getting off?"

"I am, but I'll return at one. We have folks out sick, so I'm heading home for a nap. Then back on the job. How are you holding up?"

The kindness in the nurse's voice threatened Susie's control. She had to talk around a lump in her throat. A lump that grew thicker whenever she thought of the bad outcomes. Try as she might, she couldn't put the possible loss out of her mind. "Bad and good. A mixture."

"As expected," Regina said, and then she reached out a hand to the statue and touched the angel's damp arm. "I come this way every day. I do it because I believe in God and the protection of His angels, and this statue reminds me how that belief is the strength we need in times of trouble. In times of strife."

"You need a reminder?"

Regina's expression changed. "Now and again I expect we all do. I'll be back later, all right? The little warrior is holding her own upstairs, and she took three one-ounce bottles from me overnight and then managed just under two ounces at dawn. Seems your little gal is a breakfast eater!"

Susie's heart swelled with the news. "Thank you, Regina."

"My pleasure, Susie."

Regina went toward the bus stop.

Susie turned toward the statue and murmured the little poem from Molly's crewelwork. Such a pretty verse for such a lovely child. And from that moment on, Susie left the hospital by the side door and entered the same way, stopping and praying by the angel statue each time.

Hollis came up to the hospital after work that day. He scrubbed up the way the nurse had shown them, donned a gown, and came into the nursery with Regina's permission.

He looked worn. Heartsore. He took one look at Susie and the baby and his jaw went slack. "She's no better, is she?"

"No better?" Susie looked up, surprised. "She's eaten almost two ounces twice today, Hollis. And she's taking an ounce an hour other times. Though we do have to wake her to feed her."

"Susie, I've had pups take more than that and weigh a quarter of what she weighs," he whispered in a broken voice. Hollis's family bred and raised hunting dogs. Truth to tell, he had more experience around newborns than she did, but he didn't have her experience in other matters.

"And I say we do our best to pray this baby to wellness, Hollis. She needs us in her corner, ready to fight. Ready to believe. Whatever happens, we have her now, and that's what I'm going to cling to. We have her now."

She saw the lack of faith in his face. His stance. The slackness of his hands. He stayed a little while, then went home to help his daddy with the dogs.

He could nurse an ailing pup and sit by a whelping dog, but he couldn't spare an hour for his own baby girl.

Her heart wanted to break. Shatter, even.

Then Regina crossed over to her. She peeked at the baby girl and smiled—a smile that lit up the room. She aimed that smile right at Susie and bent to look her in the eye. "We know what we're doing, Susie Stanton." She reached out and gently touched Susie's arm. "We're doing exactly what you just said, praying and tending this child to wellness, and even though some can't see her improvement, you can. And I can too." She didn't just smile at Susie then. She beamed. "That Angel of Mercy has some powerful friends up yonder. God and God alone charts our way. Amen."

She squeezed Susie's arm lightly, then went off to tend other babies. Only six lined the little nursery now. Three had gone home yesterday.

And when Susie left the hospital that night, she stopped by the statue and prayed, knowing that Regina would be there watching little Jeannine. Caring. Feeding. And singing.

And that prayer and that knowledge got her through.

Chapter Ten

"Joy, you sure do know the way to this woman's heart." Regina sighed and patted a napkin to her lips. "My old brain doesn't have the imagination to come up with so many sandwich and wrap options, each one more delicious than the next. Although I still love a Philly cheesesteak, as common as that is, but this jambalaya, sweet Lord, have mercy! That was a treat and then some. Thank you for providing supper. It was marvelous."

"Nothing common about a good cheesesteak," Joy assured her. "And it's fun to do a sampling like this, isn't it?" She'd had the Brown Dog Deli pack an assortment of sandwiches, and Shirley had arranged them onto a large platter with a generous serving of Crabby Moe's jambalaya on the side. Coffee and sweet tea rounded out the meal.

"Sure is." Evelyn stood up to help clear things, an easy task today. Shirley brought her laptop to the table as Regina moved toward the front door.

"I'm going to do a spell of settin' on the porch to see if those finches have decided to stay a while or head north like so many of their friends."

"Their pretty song is sure welcome. Do you need a sweater, Mama?"

"I'm grabbing my old one off the hook on the way," Regina replied. "Something about the comfort of a sweater you know makes things just right, now, doesn't it?"

"The older I get, the truer that is," said Anne. "Although I'm the first to tease my husband about getting stuck in a rut about what he wears."

"Predictable with age," noted Joy as she retook a seat at the table. "So Anne, what happened today that got you fired up?"

Anne filled them in. Liam had discovered Gwyneth's married name. He'd sent it to Anne and added the legal name the family had chosen when Brock Winchester went to federal prison.

Shirley typed Gwyneth's name into a search engine. It took a few false leads but eventually she brought up just what they needed. Gwyneth's married name attached to the maiden name. And her address.

Shirley tapped a finger to the table. "It's interesting that a search of her name as Winchester brings up nothing."

"So the long arm of the internet doesn't dredge up everything. I'm relieved to hear it," said Joy as she sipped her tea.

"It only knows what's been fed into it, and her daddy's conviction was prior to such widespread web-based technology," noted Evelyn. "He comes up because there have been pleas and problems in prison tied to his name. But their mother did a good job of shielding her kids by changing their name and moving away. I can't imagine how hard that would be, to have everyone in your school know that your father or mother was a felon. Kids can be mighty cruel."

"Sure can. So her married name is Lange. Gwyneth Marinetti Lange."

"Shall we stop by Mrs. Lange's place on Saturday?" Joy looked at Anne. "We can at least talk to her. Gauge her reactions. Eloise's first game isn't until eleven forty."

"Works for me," said Anne as Shirley cut wedges of the praline cake.

"I'm getting out the whipped cream just in case you need it," she told them. She grinned as she set it down on the table. "I won't deny loving whipped cream on just about everything, and Mama's pecan cake is one of my favorites."

"It melts in your mouth." Joy sighed as she tried a small forkful of the treat. "The brown sugar and pecan glaze is amazing. But the whipped cream only makes it better," she declared as she applied a generous flourish to her piece. "In for a penny, in for a pound."

Anne couldn't disagree. The sweeter weather allowed more walking time, and she loved to walk, which was good because this was the kind of cake that made walking not only a pleasure but a necessity.

Joy swung by to pick Anne up in her Mini Cooper Saturday morning. The blue car matched her eyes and was made for the Carolina coast. "I love riding in this thing, Joy," Anne said once she'd climbed in. "It makes me feel like a kid again."

"So fun!" Joy was the quiet one of the four, but she got excited over a few things. Her grandkids. Her daughter, Sabrina. Her flowers. And her car. "Wilson would have said it was too small, but then he was a big man. And there's something about the name that makes me smile every time."

They pulled up to Gwyneth Lange's home twenty minutes later. Anne wasn't sure what she expected, but the simple house surprised her. After reading up on Brock Winchester's exploits and the amount of money involved, she'd expected opulence.

Nope. Gwyneth lived in a ranch-style house on a normal, middle-class street. They parked at the curb and walked up to the small porch. Joy, looking trim and totally put together like she always did, knocked smartly on the bold black door. A black-and-white wreath with flecks of purple ribbon scattered throughout adorned the door.

"Now that's lovely," noted Joy. "I love a porch or a stoop that says welcome, and that's just what Mrs. Lange has managed here. So nice!"

The door opened. Gwyneth saw Joy first. She looked puzzled, but when she recognized Anne, her expression changed. "Who are you, and why are you here?"

"We're sorry to disturb you." Anne meant every word of it, because Gwyneth didn't look happy at their interruption. "I felt bad about our meeting yesterday. I'd obviously interrupted something I shouldn't have, and I didn't want you thinking ill of me or Mercy Hospital."

"You came here." Gwyneth stared at Anne. Stared hard. "With a friend for some kind of self-protection, I guess—"

"I'm not much protection," Joy assured her. "I'm just a friend who also loves helping folks and Mercy Hospital."

"How's your mother?" asked Anne. "I know how scary heart surgery can be."

The compassion in her voice softened Gwyneth's expression. "As well as can be expected. Barring complications, they said she could come home by the middle of the week. With rehab, of course."

"That's wonderful." Joy kept her voice low. "Anne and I have been working on a project that looks at some past cases with the

Atlanta PD. We realized you were involved in one of the cases after Anne met you yesterday. Now we understand if you don't want to talk about it at all," she continued. She raised a hand in understanding. Her deep Texas drawl added comfort to questions, as if she wasn't really prying when she was absolutely prying. "But if you wanted to share what you know, we are good listeners."

"Why are you looking into the police department?"

"Rumors," answered Anne. It was the absolute truth and just enough to ease Gwyneth's hostile gaze a little more. "Just because a case is old doesn't mean it's unsolvable."

"You two solve cases?" Disbelief colored Gwyneth's tone, and her expression matched.

"Appearances can be deceptive," answered Joy mildly. "Our outward appearance can actually be used in our favor," she continued. "Who expects two ladies of a certain age to be armchair detectives?"

"Who indeed?" Gwyneth sounded skeptical, but when she opened the door wider, Anne counted it as a victory. "Are you two friends with Liam Holden?"

"We know Liam because he worked with one of our colleagues in Atlanta."

"Then do come in, because if nothing else, you need to know the truth behind this man. What he's done and what he's capable of doing. And let me tell you, my family experienced it firsthand, so I hope you have your notebooks ready."

Anne patted her purse. She didn't carry her big bag on days off, but she had a trusty steno pad in her purse. When Gwyneth invited them to sit in a nicely furnished living room, Anne pulled the notebook out, ready to write.

"He lied about my father." Gwyneth made the statement matter-of-factly. "From the beginning. Not just him, either. There were three detectives on the case, investigating my father and his brother Brennan, two upstanding businessmen who were swindled out of a small fortune by dishonest traders. They were railroaded," she explained. "My father and uncle operated a logistics business that specialized in getting goods to people. Logistics wasn't such a huge deal thirty years ago." Despite her feelings about Liam, her voice stayed matter-of-fact as she shared the story. "But it had great potential, and my father and uncle saw that. Imagine what it would or could be now." She posed the words in a questioning tone. "You've watched the rise of delivery companies nationwide. Imagine if my father and uncle hadn't been thwarted by corporate types from an established cross-country delivery service who set them up for the fall. Big companies don't like to share profits," she went on. "When they saw the potential of Southern Express, they wanted it stopped. They did everything they could to make sure that happened."

"How so?" Anne was jotting down short, quick notes that she could check out later.

"They set them up for a crime."

"Oh my." Distress colored Joy's tone. "I'm so sorry. You're sure that's what happened?" When Gwyneth nodded, Joy pointed to Anne's notebook. "Are you getting all of this, Anne?"

"I am."

Joy redirected her calming gaze back to Gwyneth. "Go on, please."

"It was dreadful. It cast a shadow over everything Daddy did. We couldn't go to school or soccer practice or the tennis club without being followed. The FBI lurked in our bushes or just blatantly parked across the street with binoculars, those small ones like you see on TV. Watching. Waiting. Intimidating. And yet there was absolutely nothing on the books that linked the Winchester family to anything shady. The very thought of a fine, upstanding family being involved in illegal undertakings was abhorrent. Not one of us fell for the ruse, but when they invented enough evidence to put Daddy and Uncle Brennan on trial, staying near Atlanta wasn't an option. By that time the name Winchester would have spelled a long and lonely life dealing with undeserved fallout. I had to give up my friends, my neighborhood, my school."

She drew a breath. "Everything an eleven-year-old girl loves. But mostly I had to leave my NeeNee and Papa. They wouldn't leave, and they didn't want to draw attention to us by coming down here, because you know someone would have outed us if they did, so they died alone in the historic Winchester home in Atlanta. And not one of us got to say goodbye."

"I am so sorry." Joy was too. Anne heard the sincerity in her voice and read it in her face, and who wouldn't be touched by that story? "So dreadfully sorry."

"Fortunately for us, this all happened before the internet, so we were able to live a normal life here. As normal as we could without family and friends. It wasn't horrible." She leaned forward slightly, as if conceding. "We got by. But I've never stopped thinking of all we lost because bad cops told a bunch of lies."

"You said the books were solid."

"Rock solid. My father employed a wonderful accountant. He was a good man with three kids of his own and the nicest wife, so the very thought that he could or would do something wrong was unbelievable."

"Of course it was." Sympathy dripped from Joy's tone.

"Daddy was on the cusp of making it big. Maybe really big," she went on. "Not that the money was a huge deal to our family. My mother never cared. I never cared. And my siblings were younger. All they wanted to do was play and eat. Boys," she added, as if that explained everything.

"Anyway, he'd just gotten a huge contract to do an interstate system of deliveries. It was his dream come true. The culmination of so much hard work. And then along came the detectives to bring him and Uncle Brennan down. It was horrible. My mother was so proud of him. Of his hard work. She always said that her domain was in the home and his was to support the home financially. Dreadfully old-fashioned, but it worked."

Gwyneth took a deep breath. "Until they ruined it. You know how it is when they can't find the real person. They scapegoat another one so their numbers don't look bad. It's always about the numbers, Daddy said. Facts might be misinterpreted, but numbers tell the truth. I became a math teacher." She squared her shoulders. "Numbers amaze me. They're not subjective."

"No, ma'am." Joy nodded firmly. "They are objective, and there is only one right answer."

"Or a range, but yes." Gwyneth's face had relaxed as she told the story. "He liked the logistics of numbers, getting from point A to point C via B. I like the stability of them."

"And you were eleven when all this happened?" asked Anne.

Gwyneth nodded. "Yes. The boys were five and six. Well, Beau was nearly seven, actually. The police searched our house on his birthday. And found nothing, I might add."

"That had to be hard."

"When they arrested Dad and Uncle Brennan, Dad told Mom to take us away. Folks thought she went away in shame, to protect us, but he'd done nothing wrong. She knew it. We knew it. She wanted us safe, so she changed our last name to Marinetti and we moved down here. I don't look back often," Gwyneth went on. "But I did about two years ago, just to see what was happening, and there was Liam Holden with a new Charleston address. With his family. His daughter. His granddaughter. All happy and cozy with his government pension while we stayed out of sight. Out of mind."

"I'm so very sorry, Gwyneth." Anne stopped writing and met the other woman's gaze. "I truly am. Can you share a detail or two with me, though? Something we can check on? What makes you think it was a setup?"

She replied instantly. "Daddy told me."

Anne's heart sank, because the woman's look was so sincere. Either her beloved father was living a lie, or Liam was. Unless it came down to a simple and awful mistake.

"He said the government had it out for them because companies like theirs would put the postal service out of business. They were a threat, so they had to be disbanded. In order to keep them put away for a long time, they had to be accused of horrible things that they would never do."

Anne had read reports of the case. Brock and Brennan Winchester had used their fleet of delivery vehicles to move illegal firearms, drugs, and humans across the Southeast. The case against them was solid. Flush with facts and evidence, but the eleven-year-old girl had taken her father's words to heart. "What does your father say now?"

Gwyneth appeared baffled. "How would I know?"

"Visits? Phone calls? Letters?"

"He wanted us to stay away."

And they did?

Anne worked to control her expression but not quickly enough. "You think that's heartless, don't you?"

Anne shook her head. "I think families do what they need to do to survive sometimes. If your parents felt that keeping you and your brothers away from a federal prison was a smart choice, I'm not about to disagree. Prisons aren't nice places to be, and impressionable kids might have a hard time with it."

"I think a lot of inmates feel like your daddy." Joy's words helped smooth things over. "They want their children to remember them the way they were. To embrace the good times. There's not a thing wrong with that, now is there?"

"No." Gwyneth stood.

So did Anne and Joy. And then Joy reached out and touched Gwyneth's arm. "Thank you for sharing your story with us. I know it wasn't easy. And I'm praying for your mama's return to health and home. And," she said as she moved toward the door ahead of Anne, "that wreath is plumb gorgeous! And I use the word *plumb* with affection. That shock of purple in the black and white made me smile!"

"I like the black-and-white look," said Gwyneth. "The purple is for Daddy."

Joy lifted an eyebrow.

"They say he's got dementia now. He's just shy of seventy, and that's what took his daddy and every one of his uncles, so when we had this wreath made, we wanted a remembrance ribbon in it. Whatever else has gone wrong in Daddy's life, he didn't deserve that. No one does."

Anne couldn't disagree. Alzheimer's and related dementias were a growing part of Ralph's ministry visits, and they were hard. So hard. Hard on the folks who kept family home, hard on the ones who needed memory care units for help. Either way, dementia's cruel tricks and turns laid a rocky path for loved ones with the disease and those caring for them. "He'll be in my prayers. As are you," she added softly.

After Joy asked her to update them on her mother's condition and shared her contact information, Gwyneth saw them out. She closed the door gently behind them.

When they got to the car, Anne met Joy's gaze. "I was quite willing to lay the blame at her door, but I can't."

"Me neither. Of course, that would have been easy." Joy rolled her eyes.

"And the truth is rarely an easy find," Anne replied.

"You can say that again." Joy thrust the car into drive and moved out onto the road as Anne's phone chimed a text. She looked down.

The blare of a horn—

Joy's horn!

Anne snapped her attention up just in time to see a black SUV with tinted windows aimed straight for them along the quiet two-lane street.

There was nowhere to go. Joy couldn't react in time to get out of the way, and Anne's only thought was that she was glad she'd buckled her seat belt into place as soon as she sat down.

And then, horns blaring, Joy's and the other guy's, the SUV swerved off at the last second, dusting the front driver's side corner with a grazing touch.

Anne's heart pounded.

From the look on Joy's face, her heart was no better, and when Gwyneth Lange pounded on the window, Anne rolled it down, still pretty much in shock.

"What happened? Who was that? Why did they do that?" asked Gwyneth. She didn't look overwhelmed now. She looked angry. "Who would want to hurt you? Or scare you?"

Anne shook her head. "I don't know. But, Gwyneth, I can promise you one thing." She took a deep breath. "We intend to find out."

Chapter Eleven

"My heart will not stop beating," said Joy as she pulled the car into a coffee shop parking lot not far from Gwyneth's house.

"Is it too soon to point out the obvious?" quipped Anne. It took a moment, but then Joy rolled her eyes and almost smiled. But not quite.

"I meant racing, and you know it." She backed the car into a space, slipped it into park, and took a deep breath through her nose. "Talk about an adrenaline rush."

"I know. I always get one when we draw closer to the truth."

"Whereas mine come from near-death experiences," Joy responded dryly. "But you do you."

Anne reached over and gave her a quick half hug. "That too. But the fact that someone *is* trying to scare us—"

"And succeeding," said Joy, but there was a hint of cheerfulness in her tone now because they had, in fact, lived.

"—means we're getting closer. They want us off the trail," Anne insisted. "But who? And why? What do they think we'll find? And is it related to Gwyneth's family? Or Katie and Liam's family? Or something else entirely? Cops tend to make their share of enemies over time, and a good detective probably has a Rolodex of angry people. Criminals don't like being thwarted. It's possible we haven't even scratched the surface."

"I say we get coffee and bring it back to the car. I don't trust talking in the open right now," replied Joy. "I parked this way deliberately. If we have to run for our lives, I won't waste a minute backing up. It's full steam ahead, all the way."

"I like the way you think," Anne said as they approached the sidewalk.

Joy reached out for the café door and yanked it open. "It's also easier to use a car as a protective device if it's aimed forward."

Also true, and if someone would have suggested that Joy Atkins was outrageously gutsy a year before, Anne might have doubted the assertion.

Not anymore.

Joy had a backbone forged from Texas steel, but you wouldn't know it to look at her.

They got back to the car, turned the AC on, and compared notes, but by the time they'd calmed down, they realized they hadn't found out much, which made the near accident more monumental. What had they done to present a threat?

"Did someone see us with Liam and that triggered this reaction?" wondered Joy. "And, off topic, this coffee is beyond good. Or maybe gratitude for being alive is coloring my taste buds right now."

Her initial comment made Anne turn in her seat. "What about the man I saw at the hospital? The one who might have been following Liam."

"Except he wasn't." Joy squashed Anne's words with gentle pragmatism.

Unconvinced, Anne said, "The fact that Liam didn't see him doesn't mean he wasn't there."

Joy looked skeptical. "Moving in one direction or the other can't make someone a suspect."

Anne made a note on her pad. "I'm jotting him down. And if it's the same guy who kept me from falling when my bag snagged a rogue bench arm—"

"You saw this guy? Up close?"

Anne said, "I saw a man. And quite close up. He seemed nice and he kept me from falling, so I wasn't thinking about the case or Liam. But he was wearing the same kind of clothes the guy who walked behind Liam was wearing. Although jeans and a light jacket are somewhat ubiquitous around here this time of year."

"If someone is watching Liam and Katie," Joy said, "then he or she could have seen us. If they know we're helping Liam, you could be right, Anne. Clearly someone has targeted us and is warning us off."

Anne heard a ding, and Joy raised her phone and whistled lightly. "We've got ourselves a partial license plate."

"No." Anne leaned over to see the pic Gwyneth had sent, but mental red flags popped up in her brain. "How would she know to take a picture, or have her phone ready?" Doubt flooded her tone. "Unless Gwyneth was part of the attempt to scare us?"

"A most successful attempt with only temporary effect," noted Joy. The uptick in her voice meant she was ready to move on.

Another text followed. NEIGHBOR SHOT THIS THROUGH WINDSHIELD AS HE WAS RETURNING HOME BEHIND THIS GUY. BLURRY AND NOT WHOLE, BUT MAYBE A HELP? SO GLAD YOU ARE OKAY!

Anne settled back into her seat. "That makes me feel better. The thought of a random neighbor using a cell phone at the right moment makes sense. The thought of her just happening to be outside with her cell phone, ready to snap a pic, wouldn't have worked for me."

"Can you send this on to Liam?" she asked. "Let's see what he can find out through his connections."

"Normally we'd give it to the police," Joy said. "Doesn't it feel wrong to leave them out?"

Anne couldn't disagree, because it did feel wrong. And yet— "They do this all the time in mysteries. Route their way around cops."

"Fiction," Joy reminded her.

Anne bit back a sigh. She was a law-and-order person. Always had been. The thought of evading police intervention didn't sit well, but Shirley knew Liam and trusted him. "I say we follow Shirley's gut on this one. If we keep our focus on protecting Katie—"

"And lessen our focus on who's trying to kill us," interrupted Joy with pretend pragmatism.

"That is a downer," admitted Anne as Joy started the car. "Except he or she could have done serious damage and didn't, which means they're not afraid to use scare tactics but draw the line short of murder."

"In daylight." Joy turned toward the expressway leading back to the peninsula. "All I'm saying is there might be more going on than we see right now. As is often the case."

Joy drove back to Anne's car tucked in the lot not far from the hospital. Old buildings used to block her view of Mercy, but the sprawl of hospital expansion had changed the landscape significantly. She couldn't see the angel garden and the Grove from here, but the widened curve of the ER banked the near side of her view. "I know we've all got busy weekends, but should we try for an online meeting of the minds before Monday?"

Joy shook her head. "I'm swamped with cute grandkid time and Palm Sunday services. And when the soccer tournament is over, I'm taking the whole crew out for barbecue."

Joy was right. Family first. Ralph was conducting in-hospital Holy Week services in the chapel. Anne had volunteered to accompany patients down, which meant helping them back up to the units afterward. Lili and Addie had offered to help too, making their Holy Week effort even more special. "Monday, then. I'll send Liam the license plate pic and fill him in on what happened. We'll go from there. Time is short this week. But special too."

Joy sighed in agreement. "This is my favorite part of the year, my friend. See you Monday!" She waved as she headed back toward the expressway ramp.

Anne hit the unlock button on her key fob.

Then she immediately hit the lock icon with similar intensity because there, between her and the ER, was a man who looked exactly like the one who helped her at the bench. Or the one who seemed to follow Liam. Or both, if he was the same.

Common sense told her that if he had bad intentions he'd be less obvious, but there might be a brilliance aspect about hiding in plain sight.

She headed his way, keeping track of him as she moved.

He was walking easily but not strolling. His steps were intentional, as if he had a place to go but no need to hurry, two things that made him blend well. He wasn't close enough for her to get a good picture with her phone.

She had to wait to cross the street, and she was just about to step onto the crosswalk when Kitty Sue exited the ER. She'd been working the overnight but must have stayed late, a fairly common occurrence. What wasn't common was the man's reaction.

He stopped dead.

So did Anne. She paused right there on the opposite side of the street and watched while snapping pics with her phone. She pretended she was taking selfies in front of a nondescript statue but kept the camera working as Kitty Sue cut across the grass to get to the ER employee parking lot to the man's left.

Kitty Sue walked with the quick gait of youth, smiling and talking.

She was on a phone call, Anne realized, on her Bluetooth connection.

Her hands fluttered when she spoke, and as she kept moving toward her car, the man made an abrupt turn her way, as if to follow her.

Anne's heart pounded.

Traffic was streaming both ways now, typical busy late-morning congestion, and there was no way Anne could bob and weave her way across four lanes. She'd missed her chance to cross and now had no choice but to wait or cause a nasty accident. On the plus side, she was near the ER, so help would come quickly.

The downside would be stupidly risking death because she hadn't crossed with the light, which made it no choice at all. She wanted to call out to Kitty Sue, but there was no way for the young woman to hear her, and for a moment Anne feared she was about to witness something awful.

Was this Katie's stalker?

Had he mistaken Kitty Sue for Katie? Even people who worked with the women would mess up their identities from time to time, and then laugh about it. But this wasn't Katie. Did he know that? If he did, why was he following the wrong woman?

Unless Kitty Sue was the right woman?

The possibility of that bombshell reasoning made Anne's heart beat faster.

Traffic slowed as the light turned amber. Anne crossed once it was safe, but as she stepped up to the opposite sidewalk, the dynamic changed. Kitty Sue had paused by her car, still talking. She was in no hurry to get into the car, it seemed, and as she spoke, a breath of wind puffed a lock of wispy hair across her face. She reached up and gently retucked the errant hair behind her ear.

The man stopped in his tracks as if awestruck by what he saw.

So much for blending, thought Anne. As he stood there, his back to Anne, his shoulders came up. After a quick pivot, he walked away at a quick pace. He went past the ER, toward the harbor, moving with a fast, firm stride, as if all of a sudden he had places to go.

Should she follow him?

No.

Disappointment was outweighed by common sense. She was alone. Following a stranger would be foolish, and she'd promised Ralph she wouldn't be foolish. It was a promise she meant to keep.

Kitty Sue was opening her car door when she spotted Anne. "Anne, hey! Have a great weekend! I'm heading home for some sleep, I'm that dogged out."

"Well-deserved rest!" Anne called back.

Kitty Sue drove by her and, from the side, the resemblance to Katie was even stronger. Anne wasn't sure she'd be able to tell the women apart easily, except that Katie almost never wore patterned scrubs and Kitty Sue loved them. Seeing her in profile, Anne realized that it would be very easy for someone to mistake one young woman for the other if you didn't know little things about them. That had to be why the man followed Kitty Sue. He had thought she was Katie. Maybe.

But why follow Katie at all, and also follow Liam? If it was the same man? Different clothes today but similar idea. Jeans. A pullover shirt, lightweight, dark gray. No jacket with the warmer temperatures. And dark sneakers.

She crossed the street and walked back to her car. Lili was coming over with Addie, and she didn't want anything to mess up their time together. She needed to tuck this aside for a couple of days. But as she drove home, she replayed the image of the man several times. First, his reaction as Kitty Sue strolled out of the ER without a care in the world. Then, the way he drew to an abrupt halt while she nonchalantly talked at her car.

His moves suggested surprise, so had he just realized it was the wrong young woman?

She called Seamus as she drove toward North Charleston and their new-to-them home.

"Anne? What's going on?" the security head asked when he answered.

"I should probably be embarrassed or impressed that the head of security has my number in his phone," she said.

He laughed. "You're getting closer and closer to speed dial status," he teased. "What's up?"

"I was just outside the hospital and a man—who may or may not have been following Liam Holden the other day and kept me from falling when my purse went one-on-one with a park bench—started following Kitty Sue when she came out of the ER just now. My concern is that she looks so much like Katie that—"

"He might have been following the wrong young woman."

"Exactly. And then he stopped suddenly, as if realizing he was wrong. He hurried off in the opposite direction. I couldn't see his face," she continued. "I was far enough away and he never turned, so I'm not much help."

"I'll check the camera feeds," Seamus said. "What was he wearing?"

"Jeans. Gray shirt, long-sleeved. Dark shoes. Kind of shaggy hair."

"Shaggy hair," Seamus repeated. She assumed he was taking notes.

"He was heading toward the harbor when he walked away. How late does Katie work today?"

"Until six."

"Could he possibly know her schedule?" Anne wondered out loud. "Could that be why he reacted so quickly when Kitty Sue came walking out? Because he wasn't expecting Katie for hours?"

"Knowing her schedule would make him a serious stalker," said Seamus. "But if he does know her schedule, why would he be here in the middle of the day? That doesn't make any sense."

It didn't. It made no sense at all. "I'll stay late to make sure she gets home okay," Seamus assured her.

"You don't mind?"

"Of course not. Talk to you soon. And thanks for the heads-up, Anne."

"You're welcome." She pulled into her drive a few minutes later, determined to tuck errant thoughts of mystery away. Katie was in good hands, and Anne had a wonderful family weekend planned, and that was where her focus would stay. It did too, right up until Seamus texted her two shots from one of the hospital cameras.

The pictures were small, but from that camera's angle, his face came through and confirmed Anne's suspicions. The man who followed Kitty Sue was the same man who'd saved Anne from a fall earlier that week.

And maybe followed Liam?

But who was he? And what was his purpose? If it was malicious intent, he'd had multiple opportunities and done nothing so far.

So what, then, was his interest?

Anne had no idea, but one way or another, she'd find out.

Chapter Twelve

Charleston, South Carolina
Special Care Nursery
1967

"She looks good." The pediatrician finished Jeannine's examination three weeks later, and his face relaxed into a smile. "Real good. I don't know what you all are doing, but whatever it is, keep it going," he said to the nurses. "We had to fight to get funding for this little unit."

Regina knew that the tiny babies used to be portioned off in a corner of the regular nursery.

"But fight we did. Well, mothers, mostly," he admitted with a rueful smile. "They heard about better options for their babies, and they took it to the doctors, the board, anyone who'd listen. They got their wish, and we've got this. Well done." He pocketed his tiny stethoscope and peeled off his gloves. "You ladies run a tight ship, and it works. Call the Stantons and tell them the princess warrior is going home."

"I will do that." Regina got little Jeannine situated in a clean diaper and gown, and then she called Susie.

Susie and Hollis were there ninety minutes later. Hollis didn't look scared or worried now. He'd mustered up better the last week or so as the baby's health improved. "I took the whole day off," he declared as they completed Jeannine's paperwork. "I'll be back at it tomorrow, but my bosses understood. This is a special day."

"And Susie, are you returning to work?" Regina asked.

Susie finished washing up. She darted a glance to Hollis before answering. "I am. But not until the fall session of school starts. As long as Jeannine is all right. My neighbor is going to watch her three days a week, and my aunt will have her the other two. At least for now, although Aunt Ellie's daughter has just announced a baby coming this winter, so I don't know what will happen then."

"Ellie will send our peanut packing and take on her own grandchild, that's what will happen," said Hollis. "But we'll figure that out. And if you decide to stay home from teaching to raise this little one, we'll make do, Susie."

His words made Susie smile, but it was a half smile. One that didn't reach her eyes, and when Hollis went down to bring their car around, Regina took advantage of the quiet moment. "What's going on, Susie? That was a mighty nice offer, wasn't it? I know when my time comes to have a family, I'd like to scale down to three days a week."

"I don't dare stop teaching," she whispered, and Regina heard the note of desperation in her voice. "I'm pretty sure Hollis has already managed to break his vows to me. I don't dare put myself in a situation where my having no money is the only thing keeping me with him."

"He's cheating on you?"

Susie's eyes filled. Her chin quivered, but then she pushed back her shoulders and looked up. "I believe so. He may think that's just a man's way, but it's not in my house. It's something we'll work out. Or perhaps we won't. Either way, I don't dare give up my job."

It was a pickle. And a raw deal. To be married to a wonderful woman like Susie, a praying woman who took things in stride, was the kind of thing a good husband would celebrate.

But not all men were like her Charles. Not all men were good and God-fearing, and so she gave Susie a hug, then slipped her a card. A postcard. And when Susie looked at it, the beautiful image of the Angel of Mercy in the summer garden, she smiled. "This binds us together, Regina."

"It surely does, Susie." She motioned toward the door. "Let's take this baby girl down to her first chariot ride, and I'll keep both of you in my prayers. And if you'd ever want to meet up, Susie, I would like that a lot."

"Every month at least," Susie said. "We can get coffee or breakfast or even just take a walk while the weather's nice."

"Sounds good to me. And one of these days I'll have my own happy news to share," Regina declared.

"And we'll celebrate the way friends do."

They'd reached the ground floor, where Hollis was waiting in the car.

Susie took a breath. A deep one. The kind of breath Regina understood, because life wasn't always a carriage ride.

Sometimes it was a tempest, and if Susie was right about Hollis, she might have a rocky road ahead. Or maybe he'd see the error of his ways, the grace he'd been given with a God-fearing wife and a healthy baby daughter.

In any case, she'd add their situation to her daily prayers. Prayers for their marriage…for the babies and parents on the third floor…and her own quiet dream and wish for a baby of her own. Not yet. They had bills to pay and a home to buy—but then!

How they both would welcome whatever child came their way.

Chapter Thirteen

It didn't just rain on Monday morning, canceling their scheduled outdoor coffee klatch.

The heavens literally opened.

An unusually early tropical disturbance joined forces with an opposing cold front from Canada. The combination stirred up a hornet's nest of precipitation. Ominous clouds rolled in overnight. By morning the rain had set in with earnest. A day-long drizzle punctuated by more intense downpours was predicted. There was no way to meet along the waterfront with beverages, but Evelyn offered an ideal alternative. My house, she texted the group. Making coffee. Then we can drive to the hospital.

A chorus of happy emojis littered the text stream. Anne arranged to pick up Joy at her house and meet Shirley at the hospital to bring her along. Parking on Short Street was never a guarantee. Evelyn's narrow driveway only had room for two cars, but the friends knew how to make it work.

Anne had made fresh cookies for Addie's weekend visit. She packed a container and pulled up to Evelyn's at seven with Joy and Shirley. They raced up the concrete steps through the dreary drizzle. By the time they hit the stoop, Evelyn had the door swung wide. The smell of fresh coffee warmed the air.

Liam had already arrived. He was chatting with James by the coffeepot, but as the ladies piled in, James came their way. "I'm heading out," he said as he crossed the narrow hall. "Faculty meeting at eight." He kissed Evelyn goodbye and gave the women a casual wave. "I put my car on the street to give you all room," he explained as they slid off wet shoes. Then he wagged a finger, teasing. "No trouble," he ordered as he passed the four friends.

"No worries," replied Anne, and she exchanged a smile with him. James's love of history made him a perfect match for Evelyn, but like Ralph and his homilies, James's mind could wander off into history with little provocation. Evelyn said she was sure he paid attention to current events occasionally. She just wasn't sure when.

The women and Liam slipped into chairs around the table. Evelyn's house was perfect for a couple, but the narrow home didn't allow for kitchen visitors, per se. The dining room, which Evelyn and James rarely used, had coffee mugs, spoons, creamers, and sugar ready for an impromptu meeting of the minds.

Liam took the lead as Evelyn poured coffee. "I had a buddy of mine look into that partial license plate you sent me," he began.

"License plate?" Evelyn arched a brow as she filled their mugs.

"What license plate?" asked Shirley.

"Anne and I had a mini-adventure after our meeting with Gwyneth Lange on Saturday morning," Joy explained. "But with everyone's busy schedule and Palm Sunday, we didn't want to upset anyone's weekend."

"Although a near-death experience might be significant enough to share," said Liam, and clearly the wry note in his voice wasn't lost on Shirley and Evelyn. They turned toward Anne and Joy simultaneously, wearing surprised expressions.

"Near death?" Evelyn didn't get riled easily, and she liked things done in a particular fashion, but she didn't even cross to put the coffeepot back where it belonged before she took a seat, astonished. "Are you all right?"

"What happened?" Shirley's eyes went round. "And how come Liam knows about it and we don't?"

"I have connections that can look into the license plate," he replied. "And they insisted on keeping it quiet until today."

"Although we were nearly killed," Anne cut in cheerfully as she removed the plastic top from the cookie container. "But we lived to tell the tale, so there's that."

"I don't find the near or possible or even tiniest bit conceivable death of my two friends to be a laughing matter," scolded Evelyn, but she did take a cookie. "Now, tell all."

Joy filled them in on what happened and how she and Anne gave the plate photograph to Liam after their barely averted accident, which seemed not too accidental.

"It's a rental," Liam told the women. "Most likely, anyway. The SUV description and the four parts of the license plate match a rental leased out to a messenger company that keeps a fleet of vehicles for deliveries of packages, legal papers, etc.: Charleston Couriers, Inc. They specialize in things that need to be hand-delivered and kept track of every minute."

He took a sip of his coffee. "Anyway, the plate and description match one of their six vehicles. I couldn't reach anyone yesterday, but I'll see if they can tell me who had it on Saturday."

"Do you think they'd admit it if it was someone from their company?" asked Joy. "No legitimate business wants their vehicle involved in scare tactics and have anything bounce back on their corporation."

"That's true," agreed Liam. "Their business is quite lucrative, partially because of driver and messenger discretion. The last thing a company like that wants is publicity."

"And all I've got to show for my very busy and heartfelt weekend is some paint stains on an old shirt." Shirley tried a cookie and sighed. "Girl, this is melt-in-your-mouth good. I'm glad somebody in this crew likes to bake. I'm happy to sample things for you, and I consider it my privilege to taste-test whatever you bring to the table. Now, what else has happened while I was either painting or praying with Mama and Garrison?"

"Well, then there was the mysterious man outside the ER when Joy dropped me off at my car," Anne said.

Liam had lifted his coffee. He set it back down and frowned. "What mysterious man?"

Shock lifted Joy's brows. "There was? Why didn't you call me ASAP? I'd have come back to help you."

"Soccer games with cute kids are the most important ever," Anne told her. Then she explained what she'd seen.

"Maybe it's actually Kitty Sue that someone is after," mused Evelyn. "Those two have fooled folks before."

"Or is it Katie, and he mistook Kitty Sue for Katie?" asked Shirley.

"The note on the car was specific to Katie," Joy reminded them.

"True," admitted Anne. "But this man's reaction was odd." Anne folded her hands on the table. She leaned in.

"He was surprised that it wasn't Katie?" suggested Shirley.

Anne frowned. "He seemed surprised. It was like he stopped dead in his tracks. And then he just turned and walked away."

"But who is he?" exclaimed Shirley. "And why was he following Katie?"

"I don't know," Anne answered. "He walked off toward the harbor side of the hospital. Seamus checked the camera feeds outside and found two shots of him where you could actually see his face. And you're not going to believe this, but it's the same man who saved me from falling in the park area last week, although the picture is grainy."

"The one you thought might have followed Liam?" asked Evelyn.

"Exactly. I printed out the pictures." Anne reached into her bag and handed each one of them a printout. "It pixilated when I tried to blow it up more, but it might be enough for you all to recognize him if you see him again."

"See him again?" Liam's whole body was at attention. He stared at the picture in his hand. "How about seen him before?"

"You recognize him, Liam?" Anne frowned again, puzzled. "Where?"

"In Atlanta. When he testified against the mob. I've never met him in person, but I saw the trial pictures. That's Katie's biological father." He stared at the picture in disbelief then raised a surprised and fearful look to them. "What is he doing here? And more than that... What does he want?"

Chapter Fourteen

A COLD CHILL RAN DOWN Anne's spine. She stared at Liam and swallowed hard. "You said he was in witness protection."

"He was. I don't know where, or what his new identity was or is, but he's been tucked away for over twenty-five years. So why is he here? And why is he looking for Katie?"

Evelyn leaned back in her chair. "You think he is?"

"I can't imagine another reason for a man whose life is in danger to be suddenly snooping around the emergency room where his biological daughter works. How did he find her?"

Anne set her cup down. "It's almost impossible to be hidden in this day and age. Almost everyone leaves some sort of online footprint."

"Except there was nothing traceable about the adoption. Nothing at all. It was checked and rechecked, and not only by me. I made sure I had a lawyer go over everything with a fine-tooth comb to keep Katie's identity sealed. And that ancestry site hasn't sent their report yet, so how did he discover this? I would have said it was impossible."

"Perhaps because you wanted it to be impossible." Shirley kept her voice gentle. "You surely don't think this man means her harm? Not after giving her up to keep her safe."

Her words didn't calm Liam down. He scowled. "But if he's out of hiding and the mob finds him, they find her. He's practically left a trail of bread crumbs for them to follow."

"We can't know that," said Joy.

Liam sighed. "The mob has a long reach and never forgets. Most folks haven't been exposed to their handiwork. I lived it for years as a detective. You'd assume that a quarter century would put out the fires, but revenge is like code to some of these racketeers. They use it as an example to keep people in line. And they shift their illegal businesses to the crime of the day. Drugs. Gambling. Trafficking. Guns. The two men that went to prison in this particular trial weren't top tier. They were two sons of the top tier, paving their way to take command at some point. They had brothers and cousins, some who stepped in to fill the gaps their imprisonment left." Genuine worry lined his face. "I don't know what to do. I worried Sunny and Drake plenty when I explained Katie's link to the crimes, but mostly they were grateful for her father's sacrifice. Now he's here, and I don't know why or how to protect my family."

"You're worried about him? Or the mob's retaliation against him?"

"A man that sacrifices life with his child to protect her isn't likely to put her in deliberate danger now, is he?" asked Evelyn.

"Not intentionally. And yet." Liam stood. He looked determined. "His very presence could put a target on her back. I've got to find him."

"We know where to look," said Shirley. "He's been hanging around the hospital for the better part of a week, but I'm not so sure about the sacrificial part if he's been leaving her notes and stealing plants."

"Do you think he was the one trying to run us off the road on Saturday?" asked Anne. "Although how he could get his hands on a messenger car is beyond me."

"I don't know." Liam headed for the coat hooks and the door. "I need to find him. Now that I know who I'm looking for, it won't be as hard. Anne." He turned more directly toward her. "That was detective-worthy follow-through on Saturday. We just made a huge leap forward."

"Thank you." She appreciated the compliment, but the most important thing right now was to keep Katie safe. "You find him. Let us talk with the messenger company. Joy was driving, we've got the picture, and although my Texas friend may look harmless"—she flashed a smile at Joy—"she's got nerves of steel. They won't want to ignore her."

"My Wilson would have agreed with that assessment," said Joy. "Anne and I can head there later this afternoon. You focus on Katie's father," she instructed Liam as she stood too. "We'll take on Charleston Couriers, Incorporated."

Liam went out the door. The steady drum of rain intensified as the women tucked coffee clutter into the small kitchen. Once done, they slipped into their raincoats and shoes and headed to Mercy.

Anne didn't park in her free spot today. She used the parking garage with its covered access because even with an umbrella, the wind-driven rain would give her a good soaking.

They had a busy workday ahead of them, and then a visit to the messenger service offices north of them. Wet, wrinkled clothing wouldn't work for either.

She stopped by the ER after lunch. Katie was off after working long hours on the weekend, but Anne spotted Kitty Sue on the far side of the busy area. She was wearing pink scrubs dotted with fairies. When the young woman came her way, Anne complimented the scrubs. "Adorable," she said. "I don't think they get cuter than that."

"The little ones love them, but so do my older patients," Kitty Sue told her. She had the sweetest voice. Gentle and lyrical. It was one thing that set the lookalikes apart. Katie's voice was deeper and firmer. Kitty Sue's floated along, almost musical. But when they were quiet, the resemblance was startling. "I love making the older folks smile. Relaxing them," Kitty Sue continued as she made notes on an electronic tablet at the nurses' station. "They come in scared and worried, some of them wondering if this is the beginning of the end," she explained. "It's a natural question for elderly folks, so if I can wear things that make them smile and calm them down or even just change the conversation, that's a good thing. My mama always called me fairy-friendly," she added with a wink. "She said if whimsy had a name, it would be Kitty Sue, which is kind of funny because my mom isn't one bit whimsical. She's practical and pragmatic, but we get a good laugh out of our differences."

"It's funny how that works, isn't it?" said Anne. "That sprinkling of genetics."

"Well, mine is a mystery mix," Kitty Sue said. "I was adopted, and I think the fun of adoption is that you get what you get, right? My parents seem happy with me and my little brother. Most days." She added that last with a teasing smile.

"Oh, so true!" Anne laughed at Kitty Sue's explanation. "You know it's true with any baby, but adoptive parents step into the fray with open hearts and minds."

"Very true." Kitty Sue finished her notes, heard a chime, and hurried off to check it out as Shirley came up alongside Anne.

"I told Garrison what's going on with Katie," she whispered, chin down so they wouldn't be overheard at the busy nursing station. She pretended to be engrossed in something on a tablet.

"You two had lunch together again?"

There was no denying a hint of rosiness in Shirley's cheeks. "PB&J with a side of apple slices, that new Cosmic Crisp apple that stays so well in the fridge."

"You're dating one of Charleston's most eligible bachelors and we're talking about apple slices?" Anne smiled at Shirley's discomfiture. "I know you don't want to create potential problems, but two adults should be able to see one another without major repercussions."

"And yet there's nothing wrong with employing discretion," Shirley replied. "For a bit. Garrison is administration. I don't want repercussions for either of us if this isn't a forever-after kind of deal. Right now we just enjoy each other's company from time to time. Let me add, though, that he is a wonderful man."

"There's logic and hope in that." Anne's pager chimed. She hurried toward the discharge area and headed up the silver elevators. She worked discharge the rest of the day, and when she met Joy at three fifteen, they grabbed coffee from the in-house coffee kiosk and headed to Anne's car. By three forty they were parked outside an almost meek office tucked on the back side of a nice strip mall just shy of North Charleston. The nondescript setting offered a nothing-to-see-here vibe, but there were three black SUVs parked facing forward. The tinted windows and the model matched the

SUV that had nearly hit them two days before. Anne snapped pics of the three vehicles. Not one of them carried the partial plate they had a picture of, but that wasn't a big surprise.

They walked inside the small office.

An elderly woman was seated at a desk-like counter. Behind her was another office door. She looked up and smiled when they entered. "Good afternoon. How can we help you ladies?"

Anne let Joy take the lead because it was her car that was involved with the near accident. "This," Joy said to the woman. She held her phone up, and the picture of the SUV was splayed across the screen. "This SUV nearly hit me on Saturday. I was angling out onto the street and this SUV, with plates that partially match one of the SUVs in your fleet, aimed right for me at a high rate of speed. A witness caught this photo and sent it to me."

"I'm so sorry." The woman seemed genuinely concerned. She leaned over and examined the photo. "That is very much like the vehicles we use, but no one was using our delivery service on Saturday. We do occasional Saturday deliveries, but there was nothing scheduled this past weekend."

"And yet pictures don't lie," said Joy. She kept her voice mild but firm. "There are no other black SUVs with these four digits in the state system, which means it was one of your vehicles that tried to intimidate us on Saturday. Unless your vehicle has been stolen? Or your plates were stolen?"

The door to the back office opened. It had a frosted window so that nothing could be seen through the glass. A middle-aged man came through the door. He moved forward and flanked the woman. "What's going on?"

Joy reiterated what she'd just said. He shook his head. "My fleet was here in the parking lot all weekend. We had no deliveries."

"Do you have cameras?"

He frowned. "We do."

"Can you check the feed from Saturday?"

The frown deepened. His jaw twitched, and he began shaking his head.

Joy waggled her phone. "I don't take attempts on my life lightly, sir, and I hope you don't either. I can go to the police, but I thought it was smarter to come straight to you when I realized that you run a solid but sensitive business here."

The frown eased slightly. "That is our goal."

"Which is why we're here," Anne assured him. "When we realized where the SUV was from, it seemed odd for someone in a quiet business to do something so brash with a company vehicle."

"Give me a minute." He went back into his office and returned quickly. He came to the counter and splayed his hands. "Not us, ladies, I'm happy to say."

He tried to look happy, but Anne saw the worry in his eyes. He was lying. She sensed it, and she was pretty sure Joy did too.

"None of your vehicles left the lot on Saturday?"

He shook his head firmly, but then Joy went one step further.

"And by that you mean that all of them were in the lot all day Saturday."

A muscle near his jaw twitched again. "I told you that nothing left the parking area on Saturday."

"And everything was parked there on Friday night?" asked Anne.

The narrowing of his eyes raised Anne's suspicions. "Someone kept a vehicle over the weekend," she mused.

He ran a hand over his jaw and nodded. "Yes. Which means I was derelict in my duties on Friday, because I had a courier's word that the vehicle in question would be parked and locked before midnight. It was here when I came in this morning, and my son had his confirmation this weekend, so I never even looked at the camera feed. Was anyone hurt?"

"No. Shaken, yes." Joy faced him directly. "He aimed right for us. I was driving a Mini Cooper, and he was driving a tank-sized SUV. Saying I feared for our lives is no exaggeration. So now the question is, who was driving that vehicle Saturday morning?"

He shook his head. "I will find out. We run a reputable business here. Trustworthy employees are a huge part of that. The employee who had the vehicle is on paternity leave. His wife delivered a baby boy Saturday morning."

"That's quite a distraction."

"And a solid alibi," added Joy. "If he can prove he was with her at the time. At any rate, someone was driving that vehicle on North Lattimore that day. I know because it almost killed me."

She gave the shop owner her name and number, and when they got back to Anne's car, Joy whooshed out a breath. "I nailed that."

Anne laughed. "You sure did. Small but mighty. And it's an interesting twist, isn't it? That an employee whose wife goes into labor doesn't return the vehicle and yet it gets used to frighten us."

"Someone connected with that employee?" Joy reasoned.

"It sounds likely."

"But why would they think it wouldn't be traced?"

"Because they came at us full frontal?" suggested Anne. "South Carolina doesn't have license plates on the front, so there were no identifiers from our vantage point. He or she got unlucky."

Anne drove back to Joy's house while Joy texted the group what they'd discovered. She read the responding texts back to Anne, and by the time Anne pulled up into Joy's driveway, everyone was informed.

Joy didn't climb out right away. "I've got a question for you. It's been bothering me all day," she admitted.

"What is it?"

"Why would Katie's biological father show up out of the blue like this?"

Anne had been wondering the same thing.

"Liam said she sent a sample to a DNA site and that the results weren't in yet," Joy continued. "But I'm worried, Anne. What if Liam's the dishonest one? What if the DNA results *are* in and this man's baby was taken from him all those years ago? I want to believe Liam, but this timing stretches credibility. And if that is Katie's father and Liam is out looking for him, what would Liam do to protect his family?" Worry lines formed between her brows. "I want to trust Shirley's instincts on this, but after listening to Gwyneth on Saturday and now realizing that this is Katie's real father searching for her, well"—she lifted her shoulders—"I'm worried we might be trusting the wrong person."

Chapter Fifteen

Charleston, South Carolina
Summer 1969

"Susie, I can't get over how big she is! Hey, Jeannine!" Regina bent low and smiled into Jeannine's big blue eyes. She'd been pretty bald the last time they'd gotten together. Now a wreath of wispy blond curls framed the little one's china-doll face. "Oh my word, think of how little she was. And those early days, how we prayed, and look at how those prayers were answered."

Susie had tucked Jeannine into a stroller because the only way they'd get a moment's peace would be to keep the stroller and the busy toddler moving. "I'm so glad you were able to meet us today, Regina. Now that school's out for the summer, I have more time, but I never meant to go this long without visiting."

"Oh girl, we are both busy," Regina told her. "Working. Living. Getting things done. You know my mama's been needing some extra hands these days."

"And you are a blessing for helping out," Susie told her.

"On top of that, we're moving into our place next week," breathed Regina with a sigh of relief. "It's been our goal and our dream, one of them, anyway, and to get that piece of our own personal pie over there in Mount Pleasant is a goal met. Close to Mama and the folks I grew up with, although that new interstate is changing things up fast."

"They want every state connected, north, south, east and west, and that's an amazing thing to think about, isn't it? When I teach about railroads and planes, we talk about traveling. My seventh graders are full of stories and hopes and dreams, but the thought of these big roads linking everyone amazes me. Think how many folks have a couple of cars now, when we grew up with one that didn't work half right. Of course, Miss Molly didn't drive. It was Aunt Ellie that had the car. Still, so much change. And then." She gave Regina a sideways smile. "Once you have that house, I expect I'll hear news at long last, Regina."

"I'll shout that news from the housetops." Regina laughed. She and Charles both loved children, and getting a home of their own was another step toward that dream. "Goals set and met and new ones coming. How is our Miss Jeannine doing? All is still well?"

"Fine and fit and a treasure." Susie's smile dimmed. "Though we'll be saying goodbye to Miss Molly soon. I had her to the clinic last week, and the cancer's taken hold. Taken hold bad. She's getting some treatment, but she'll be coming home in two days. I wanted to get our visit in beforehand because there won't be much time after I have her back home."

"Is she staying with Ellie?"

"She's staying with me," Susie replied. "I put my foot down when Hollis squawked, because he's always got something to fuss over. Molly Abernathy raised me from little up, and I won't let her go home to God alone. I just won't."

"If you need help, Susie, I'm available. I'm not an elder nurse, but I've helped Mama enough to know how far tender loving care goes when folks get ready to meet their Maker."

"I might take you up on that," said Susie. "But it's a long bus ride over my way, and a transfer to boot."

"We have a car."

Susie's eyes went wide. "You did it!"

Regina laughed. "Yes, we did. We've been saving and saving, and two weeks ago we went out and bought ourselves one of those Plymouths. Practical. Charles doesn't take to fancy, although I said cloth seats, because no one in their right mind should live in the South and get those vinyl seats that stick to your legs."

"That's an upgrade."

"It was, but it made sense to me. And I'll still take the bus to work. It's direct and easy, even from the new place."

"Oh, Regina, I'm so happy for you!" Susie stopped the stroller to give Regina a hug. Jeannine peered around, peeking at them, and when she saw them hugging, she extended her arms. "Me! Me! Me!"

"Oh, you sweet precious, of course we'll hug you too." Regina and Susie bent low and hugged the little one from both sides as the warm sun bathed the walkway stretching next to the water. A sweet breeze ruffled Regina's skirt, and it felt good. So good! Good to be young, filled with dreams, and in love.

Wasn't she so, so blessed?

Chapter Sixteen

ANNE WORKED TO RELAX HER grip on the wheel because Joy had voiced the concern she felt. "I know what you mean. About Liam. If we go on gut, then I say we trust him and help his cause. But if we go on timing, the coincidental factors don't seem possible." She tapped the steering wheel. "Katie's working tomorrow."

Joy nodded.

"I'm going to ask her about the DNA thing. She'd mentioned it to Shirley while I was in the area, so I heard her say she was doing it, but that's all I know. If she did it a while ago, we have our answer, and we know that test brought her father here because she asked to be linked to relatives. If she did it more recently, then we know Liam's telling the truth. But then what brought her father here? Because I don't believe in coincidences either. At least not in general."

"It's a plan." The rain had stopped, but the dank gray day was still unpleasant. Joy hurried to her door and when she let herself in, Anne backed out and drove home, mulling.

Ralph had made an easy supper of pork tenderloins and mushrooms over rice. He'd done more cooking this past year than he had in his entire life, and not only did Anne appreciate the effort, he was getting good. "This is amazing," she told him after just two bites. "What a treat to come home to good food. Thank you, darling." She leaned over and feathered a kiss to his stubbled cheek.

He grinned. "You're most welcome. When you said you and Joy were going off to meet with someone, I realized I probably wouldn't see you for a bit."

She grinned. "True." She explained what had happened that day, how Liam had recognized Katie's father and how the SUV hadn't been returned to the fleet Friday night as promised.

"Did you ask where the messenger's baby was born?"

She hadn't even thought of such a thing. "No. My bad."

"They might have been right there at Mercy," Ralph suggested. "Depending on circumstances, maybe they still are, but you don't want to use your position there to corner people."

He was right. That would be an abuse of power. Not that Anne had power, but she had proximity, and she wouldn't use that to her advantage with a patient.

Staff?

Yes.

Patient?

No. She couldn't do that in good conscience.

She, Ralph, Lili, and Addie would be working over the holiday weekend, helping folks to Easter services in the chapel before they'd enjoy dinner together, but when she heard that Regina's stove broke down on Wednesday with no repairs available for nearly a week, Anne invited them to Easter dinner while she and Shirley were having lunch near the Angel of Mercy. "You know it's more fun to cook for six than four," she told Shirley honestly. "I love it when we have a gang around, and that doesn't happen so much now that Ralph's retired. Say you'll come."

Shirley hesitated. Then she drew a breath. "We were going to have Garrison over for dinner, though."

"The more the merrier," declared Anne. But when she read Shirley's expression, she paused. "You don't think he'll want to come? Good night nurse, the guy likes us, and it's not as if we're taking out a billboard sign saying Shirley plus Garrison. It's ham. Fairly delicious and mundane." She grinned and gave Shirley an elbow poke.

"I'm being silly, aren't I?"

"You like your privacy. You don't want a public breakup. And you love your job. All reasons to be discreet, but the beauty of Easter Day is in the celebration. So explain to Garrison, and if your sweet mama could make a salad, that would round things out beautifully."

Shirley gave her a quick half hug. "I'll do it, Anne, and it'll be fun. Heaven knows most of Mother Emmanuel's congregation has us getting engaged at any moment, and you know the older folks don't have much of a filter. They say what they think, and more than one has let me know that I should grab hold and hang on while the bloom's still on the rose."

"No." Anne lifted both brows. "Shirley, did someone say that?"

"A couple of someones, truth be told, and at forty-four years old, there's some sense to the advice." She laughed. "And they don't let up on Garrison, either. When one of the old dears mentioned how good we looked together—"

"In your paint-flecked jeans," noted Anne, grinning.

"Exactly." Shirley's smile deepened. "Garrison held my hand all the way to the car." Her eyes twinkled. "And...he kissed me. Right in front of them."

"Oh, Shirley." Anne hugged her full-on this time. "I'm so happy for you."

"I am too, but I don't want to assume anything. There are a couple of rough breakups in my past, Anne." She gazed up at the angel statue. She didn't sigh, but the pensive expression revealed her emotions. "I came here to help Mama. After some rough personal moments back in Atlanta, I certainly didn't entertain illusions about romance and happily ever afters. I'm all right with going slow."

A pastor's wife witnessed a lot of broken relationships in her role, so Anne understood Shirley's hesitation. "Nothing wrong with day by day," she replied. "You know a river runs deep and strong as it flows downhill to a lake or a sea." Anne gazed up at the statue too. Then she shifted her focus back to Shirley. "But it doesn't start that way, my friend. It starts as a bunch of little creeks and streams and run-offs that slip this way and that, finding their way until they unexpectedly meet up. Their paths may be different, but when they merge, the combination is a force to reckon with. That's how I see love. And if that's what happens with you and Garrison, then I'm truly happy for both of you."

"You make me blush," Shirley scolded lightly. "And smile. I've never liked being the center of attention."

"But being the center of one man's attention is a pretty sweet thing," said Anne.

"It is, and I've learned to expect the unexpected." Shirley popped her lunch sack back into her slightly larger satchel as Joy came their way. "They've asked me to stay late tonight."

"You'll miss your ride," said Anne.

"I texted her to go ahead without me. Garrison offered to see me home. I'll be here until nearly seven, but he said he'd catch up on paperwork."

"A nice way to end the day, I'd say." Joy gave Shirley a shoulder nudge.

Shirley smiled at them before she started for the doors. "You know it is."

"I came out for a quick walk," Joy told Anne. "Do you have time?"

"Almost twenty minutes."

"Perfect." Joy looked around the space and smiled. "I'm really starting to love this place. Except for the lack of football. I did enjoy football with Wilson."

Anne tucked her small bag over her shoulder. "There's always something to miss, isn't there? And to remember."

"Sure is." They exchanged smiles and started toward the water. The breeze and shady trees afforded a coolness that would be scarce soon, so catching that fresh air now was a blessing. They got halfway down the walk when a familiar form came their way.

Katie's father.

He wasn't walking casually. He was moving with purpose. As he drew closer, she wasn't sure if they should run, scream, do both, or greet him.

He spared them the trouble of making a decision. "I'm not here to hurt anyone."

Anne speared him with a look. "Is that supposed to reassure us? We know who you are."

He frowned. "The detective told you. I saw you with him. You're helping him."

She didn't reply.

"I don't want to see him. Talk to him. I can't trust anyone from the police. I don't dare."

Liam had said the same thing, but Anne let it go for the moment. "You came here because of a DNA match."

He frowned. "I have no idea what you're talking about."

"Katie sent a sample to an ancestry site to track her DNA and find lost relatives. That's how you found her, correct?"

The creases in his forehead deepened. "I've been in witness protection for twenty-five years. Why would I risk all I've given up to have someone track my DNA online? I've never been to an ancestry site."

Joy frowned. "If you didn't come here because of Katie's DNA, why are you here? What brought you?"

"Her heart. Their hearts, actually."

Joy and Anne exchanged glances. Anne spoke first. "I don't understand."

"My wife died shortly after childbirth. She died from a congenital defect they thought was resolved in childhood. I didn't realize it until I read recent research about it. My late wife's mother probably had the defect too in some form. She managed to live into her forties. My wife was fine until she gave birth to our second daughter twenty-five years ago. She suffered a major heart episode and died when our little girl was four days old."

Something wasn't adding up. Literally. "But Katie's twenty-seven," Anne said. "Your timing is off by a couple of years."

He frowned. "A man doesn't forget when he lost his wife, ma'am. And I'm not sure what you mean, because I surrendered both girls so they would never be found by the mob. The only thing I had when I left South Dakota was the knowledge that the adoptive family lived in Charleston. I came here on the chance they might still be here. I don't want to mess up their lives. I just want them safe."

Anne didn't dare look at Joy. She posed the next question with a lightness she didn't feel. "What do you mean 'their lives'?"

"My daughters. Emily and Amelia. Both given up for adoption when I went into witness protection, because I didn't want to take a chance on the mob finding me."

Two daughters?

Anne looked at Joy now and read similar surprise in her eyes. "But you're taking a chance now?"

"Only long enough to make sure they realize the danger of this heart condition. It doesn't show up on standard tests. If it had, their mother would still be alive. But it doesn't, and if the doctors don't go in and repair the problem, it's a heart attack waiting to happen. When I realized the gravity of the situation, I had to find them or their families just long enough to make sure they knew. I couldn't live with the thought that one or both of them might have this undiagnosed defect and I didn't try my best to let them know."

Anne was still attempting to wrap her head around the knowledge that there were two girls. Not one.

"How do you know all this?" asked Joy.

"I married a cardiologist in South Dakota," he told them. "Brenna was the one who delved into the defect, and then into Jeannine's records in Atlanta. That's where we lived," he told them. "Until life turned upside down. But that's in the past," he said firmly. "All I want to do is make sure my girls' futures are in good hands."

"You said you have two daughters."

He turned toward Anne. "Emily was two when I relinquished them. Amelia was five and a half months. It was by far the worst experience of my life. Every day I've wondered if I ran scared or did the right thing. And every day I come up with the same answer. I don't know. It's funny that they both chose medicine, and yet understandable. Their mother was a nurse."

They both chose medicine.

It all suddenly made sense while making no sense at all as Anne remembered his reaction to Kitty Sue on Saturday. Did he think Kitty Sue and Katie were his girls? Did he think they were sisters?

Anne's pager pinged.

She winced. "I have to get back to work."

"Me too." Joy was clearly as reluctant as Anne to end the conversation. "When can we meet again? Talk this through?"

"Without the detective? I didn't work with him, but I recognized him from Atlanta. The cops that helped me were great. But mob money has turned law enforcement heads in the past. I'm taking no chances."

"If you're right, you're talking about his grandchild, and I don't think he'd do anything to hurt her or put her in danger. And he's got background none of the rest of us do," added Anne sensibly. "You trusted the police enough to get you safely put away. Liam Holden has way too much to lose here. I think you should let him come and listen. Maybe between all of us we can figure this out. The primary goal is to keep people safe, isn't it? And if your questions and searching have rekindled mob interest, then we can't afford to leave Liam out of the loop."

Joy took a step back. "We've got to get to work."

"This afternoon. Waterfront Park? So we're not so obvious."

"The detective will be with us," Anne warned him. "Or none of us will come."

He flashed her a look of understanding, as he had that first day when he kept her from falling. "I made a huge sacrifice that put a target on my back. A target I directed away from my family. If Brenna hadn't discovered this problem, I'd have stayed hidden. You think my search has caught the mob's interest? I don't know how that could have happened. I tried to contact the lawyer that handled the girls' adoption, but he must have retired. No one knew anything about him, so I came on my own. Whoever sealed those records did a good job. A hint of this and that brought me here. To Mercy Hospital. And my girls."

This man seemed sure that Kitty Sue and Katie were his daughters. "We'll see you this afternoon. Five thirty." That would give Evelyn and Liam time to come with them if they were available.

"I'll be there. By the pier," he said.

As they turned back toward the hospital Joy said, "This is a pickle, Anne. He thinks Katie and Kitty Sue are his daughters. Just because they happen to look alike."

Her words made Anne stop in her tracks. "What if they *don't* just happen to look alike?"

Joy rolled her eyes. "I think you're clutching at straws, my friend."

Joy was probably right. The idea was preposterous because things like that just didn't happen anymore. Did they?

Kitty Sue had said she was adopted.

As Anne signed in for the afternoon, her mind kept one thought spinning.

What if the young women's resemblance wasn't a coincidence at all? What if they really were the man's daughters?

Chapter Seventeen

Charleston, South Carolina
Summer 1970

Susie got off the bus a few blocks from Regina's address.

Hollis had told her not to go. Hollis liked that Regina had helped save his baby's life, but that was her job, after all, not Susie's, and that was that in his book.

When she'd needed help with Molly the year before, Regina had shown up with willing hands again and again. Hollis hadn't liked that much, either, but he wasn't missing tee times to care for the only mother Susie had ever known.

Other folks came around to offer their assistance and say goodbye. The *Evening Post* had even done a write-up on Molly, because she'd raised the bar high for so many.

Susie hurried up the little walkway, climbed the three steps, and knocked on Regina's crisp white door. And when her heartbroken friend opened the door, Susie grabbed her in a hug. The kind of woman-to-woman hug that meant so much.

"Now you sit and let me take care of you for a change," Susie bossed when they got into the cozy little kitchen. "Regina, this place is just beyond cute, cute, cute! You've got an eye for welcome, that's certain."

"Thank you." Regina sat down heavily in one of the chairs. The seats didn't match, but they looked right together, like a scene from the Three Bears. A papa bear chair. A mama-sized one. All that was missing was the dream: a baby-sized chair.

"Are you feeling all right?" Susie set tea to steep, then crouched in front of Regina. Some folks shrugged off pregnancy loss as a "better luck next time" kind of situation. Not Susie. She reached out and hugged Regina again, then whispered, "I am so sorry, my friend. So very sorry."

Regina crumpled.

Tears flowed.

And Susie held tight like Regina had held her three years before. She let the tears fall, she grabbed tissues by the handful, and she made the bracing hot cup of tea, because this being a woman thing—being a mother—was a tough, tough business.

"I'm sorry. I thought I was over this." Regina fluttered the clutch of tissues in her hand before bringing it to her face. "Then it sweeps in like a wave, Susie. A big, crashing wave, a tsunami, and hits me full force. Because I'm not young."

"Oh, darling, you're not exactly ancient, either."

"In baby years, things get tougher as you go on," Regina replied. "I knew that, I knew the statistics. It's my job to understand these things, and still we waited until things were right. Just right. As if we could dictate the timing to our bodies. My body, actually." Dismay dragged her features. "Why did we think it was smart to wait?"

"Wait or not, losing a baby is something that can happen anytime. Anytime at all. You know this. You've had young mothers miscarry. And older ones."

"I know." Regina gripped the edge of the table. "I'm mad at myself. I know better than to think everything goes fine. I see it all the time. So why am I so surprised and broken because things didn't go right with us? This time?"

"Because it's not about what you know, Regina." Susie stayed there, crouched at her friend's feet. "It's what you feel. We mamas attach to that baby from the start, and a good thing too, or we wouldn't be putting ourselves through it, now would we? We wouldn't take the risk, but from the time that little one takes hold, he or she is ours. Oh, they belong to their daddy too, but it's not the same, because it's us turning green when folks fry sausage, us watching our ankles swell and our belly grow so big we can't even see our feet. Don't feel bad about feelin' bad," Susie implored. "I'd be more worried if you weren't wretched over this. You and I feel things. We feel them deep. And I'm just so sorry that you have to go through this."

She hugged Regina again.

Any person raised by Molly Abernathy didn't look at the outside. They looked at heart and soul and goodness and need. That's the way Susie was raised. And that's how their dear Jeannine would be raised too. "Oh!" She stood quickly. "I almost forgot! Look what I found on my camera, Regina!"

She reached into her handbag, withdrew a 4 × 6-inch print and handed it to Regina. "Remember when that woman said she'd take our picture by the angel statue? And then I forgot to get that roll developed, but look how good this came out."

The shot was a close-up of the two of them beside the Angel of Mercy. They stood in full sun, but a trick of shoreline fogging obscured the buildings behind them, leaving the background misted and the two women in the foreground brightly defined. "Funny how we're in the light, isn't it? While everything else is trapped in fog." A shiver didn't snake its way down her arms. It shot down, as if the picture's disparity meant something, which was ridiculous, of course.

Regina sighed and smiled as she saw the picture. "I do love this." Her smile deepened. She held the picture up, then close to her heart. "I'll treasure this always. And how is the little warrior doing?"

"Amazing," declared Susie. She opened the plastic container she'd toted along. "Brownies," she said. "With frosting. Homemade, because Molly would turn over in her grave if she saw me buying canned icing." She tapped the square container. "I know it doesn't help," she added softly, "but being friends does. Knowing we're in this together, Regina. And praying for the next time."

She clutched Regina's hand.

Regina covered Susie's hand with hers, and when Susie offered a prayer, Regina's tears dried.

She brought her chin up, and she raised her cup of tea to Susie's with a quiet *clink!* "To next time. God willing."

The toast was a signal to move forward, something these two women knew a lot about. Susie nodded. Smiled. And raised her mug. "God willing."

Chapter Eighteen

ANNE HURRIED BACK TO WORK after leaving Joy. She tried to put the situation out of her mind. That worked while she was helping patients to the discharge loops, but when there was a short lull late afternoon, she stopped by the ER.

Katie and Kitty Sue were both working. Anne wanted to see them together through a different mindset. Not as colleagues who happened to look alike but as possible sisters. When she rounded the corner, Katie was jotting notes. She looked up, saw Anne, and waved her over. "One mystery solved," she said softly. "The note on my car."

"The spooky, unsigned 'Good morning, Katie' message?"

"That's the one." The cheerful tone of Katie's voice underscored her relief. "Drew Mason. The EMT. He thought it was weird that I never acknowledged the message, so he asked me about it this morning."

"How does one acknowledge an anonymous note?" asked Anne sensibly.

"There was a signed coffee card attached," explained Katie. "Someone stole the card but left the note. I won't pretend I don't feel like someone is still watching me. And not Drew Mason." She glanced around to make sure no one else was listening. "Seamus said a dark SUV pulled out behind me on my way home the other night. It turned off right before my street. He said he doesn't know if it was a deliberate follow or coincidence, but the person may have realized Seamus was following him while he was following me."

Another dark SUV? Or the same one that threatened them on Saturday morning? Dark SUVs were plentiful throughout the Charleston area. "I don't like that."

"Me neither, but it's definitely less unnerving when I have an armed escort ensuring my safety."

"A swoon-worthy one at that." Kitty Sue came up in time to hear the last part of Katie's explanation. "And I think Drew's a catch, so maybe I'll bat my eyelashes in his direction now that you're out of the picture."

Katie winked. "Bat away. He's a good guy."

"But he's not Seamus," Kitty Sue whispered when she spotted Seamus coming around the corner.

There was no mistaking Katie's blush.

He came straight their way and set a candy bar on the nurses' counter. He didn't try to hide it or pretend he wasn't flirting. "Your favorite."

Katie was obviously surprised. "How do you know that?"

He tapped the bar and gave her a knowing look. "Your Facebook page. I can't see all your posts, because we're not friends, but I can see some of your friends' pages and your replies to them. About candy. Work hours. Your ancestry search." He frowned. "And when you're expecting a day off."

"Oh man." Katie frowned. "I didn't know anyone could randomly see that."

"Not random, necessarily, but friends of friends," he told her. "And some of your friends are quick to accept friend requests from good-looking guys."

"You did that?" she asked, and her voice squeaked a little.

"I used file pics. Not my own. And a phony name. But yes, they took the bait quick, which means that anyone else that wants to 'see' you without being seen can do the same thing. It's a simple matter of following the social media trail. I wanted you to know that it doesn't take a lot for someone to discover things about us. Things we think only a few can see."

"I hate that I never thought of it that way, because I should have," Katie replied. "But I'll still accept the candy bar."

"There's two." He slipped one to Kitty Sue too. "I wasn't able to get around your friends quite so easily," he told Kitty Sue. "Only one picked up the bait."

"They're younger and not as desperate," she teased.

Katie skewered her with a look. "I'm not desperate."

"Of course you're not. Why would you be?" Seamus smiled at her—just her—and began to walk away. When he'd rounded the corner, Kitty Sue bumped Katie with her elbow.

"I'm considering this open season for me to get to know the EMT," she whispered. "Just to see."

Katie was sitting. Kitty Sue was standing, leaning down. Katie looked up and Kitty Sue looked down and when they exchanged smiles, Anne was pretty sure she saw what Katie's father had seen on Saturday.

It wasn't just a similarity in looks. That was a common enough coincidence.

It was their mannerisms. The tilt of the head, the way they angled their chins while listening to someone, and even the habit of using their left hands to support their chins when thinking.

But if he was right and these girls were more than colleagues, how had this happened?

Anne had planned on getting a few late-day errands run, but unexpected discharges messed that up. Fortunately, she had tomorrow off and would have time to gather those last-minute Easter dinner necessities and a few more milk chocolate bunnies. Not for Addie. For Ralph. He loved those things, and she enjoyed making him smile.

A call from Joy came in as Anne hurried to collect her things at the end of the day. "Gwyneth phoned to make sure we're all right."

"Really?" That put a firm check in the "nice person" column by Gwyneth's name.

"She said the whole thing shook her up, and she wanted to make sure we were okay. I assured her we were. I didn't mention how we followed up on it. Just in case the sincerity wasn't all that sincere."

"That was nice of her, and smart of you."

"Thank you. When I hung up with her, I looked up Lee Spencer's address. Do we have time to pop over there after our five thirty meeting?"

"I can't tonight. Ralph needs help with a backyard project, but what about tomorrow? You and Shirley and I are all off tomorrow."

"First thing? I'm watching the girls later in the day before the Maundy Thursday services."

"That would be perfect. Then I can get my errands run. You've got the address?"

"I do, and I purposely called you now so that I could ask when the men weren't listening."

Anne grinned. "I like how you think, my clandestine friend. We don't want to assume anything."

"Exactly. I'll text Shirley. See you in five!"

They met Liam and Evelyn at the angel statue and walked to Waterfront Park a few minutes later. The park's fountains were a draw for tourists and locals, but Anne loved the big, broad pier, and how it stretched out into the water. The rhythmic trolling of gliding or chugging ships soothed her. The movement of the water and the boats seemed strengthened by the steadiness of land. The elongated row of covered benches, swings, and tables lining the pier invited folks to sit and let the peace of God's nature seep into their bones.

She spotted the man at the second set of covered benches. She turned toward Liam. "Liam. What's this guy's name? We never introduced ourselves."

"Kevin Eddington. He was a lawyer in Atlanta for several years before his life turned upside down. All from being in the wrong place at the wrong time."

"The bad guys went to jail?" asked Anne.

"For life," Liam answered softly. "No parole."

"Then maybe he was in the right place after all."

Liam didn't look convinced. "He made really rough sacrifices. I've often wondered if I would be able to do it if our situations were reversed. And my answer is usually no."

Liam moved forward. He drew up to the taller man. "Kevin Eddington, correct?"

The man nodded.

Liam extended his hand. "Liam Holden. Former—"

Kevin Eddington interrupted him. "Atlanta detective. I remember. I recognized you right away. The girls have changed a lot. You haven't. Although the hair's thinner up top."

Liam frowned. "Girls?"

Eddington acknowledged the three women with a quiet nod, then led the way over to the next covered section of the broad concrete pad. Swings and tables offered shady repose where the pier jutted out into the water. He didn't sit, so they stood with him. "Emily and Amelia."

Liam's expression deepened. "I don't understand."

It was Kevin Eddington's turn to frown. "My daughters. I saw one of them call you Gramps last week."

"Katie."

The name put a measure of hurt into Eddington's eyes. He blinked it back. "I didn't think how hard it would be, hearing their new names. New lives. I just wanted to make sure they were safe."

"By showing up here with a possible target on your back?" Liam kept his tone questioning, not critical.

"If I could've found an easier way to do this, I would have," Kevin replied. "It took weeks of hunting down dead ends, twists and turns. Their adoptions were well cloaked, just like we planned, but the legal office didn't redact the full word *Charleston* from one of the papers, so this was a good place to start. And then to realize they were still here was a blessing. I don't want to stir things up."

"Too late for that. Someone is already making Katie nervous," Liam told him. "But back up the train," he continued. "You keep saying 'they.' We adopted one little girl. One beautiful, amazing, and healthy little girl that my daughter and son-in-law named Katie. And they didn't live anywhere near Charleston then, so I'm not buying the whole unredacted Charleston story."

Eddington's jaw firmed. He glanced from Liam to the women. "I have two daughters. Emily had just turned two when I decided to testify. Amelia was a baby. A little over five months old. The sweetest things you've ever seen, and seeing them now, they are the image of their mother. She'd have loved knowing they both become nurses. Each doing a job she admired. So if you adopted Katie, who adopted Amelia? And why were they split up?" Anger swelled his voice. He glanced around, then turned the volume down a notch. "That wasn't part of the deal. The only thing they had was one another after losing their mom and me. Who would do that?"

Liam's confusion didn't seem feigned. "I don't know. To add another layer of protection? Invisibility? I had no idea there were two girls, Kevin. None. And I know my daughter would've loved to have both. Having Katie in our family has been the best gift we could ever imagine. But there was no option for two girls, or we'd have taken it."

The distraught look on Kevin's face broke Anne's heart. Evelyn's and Joy's expressions mirrored hers. Why would someone have done such a thing? "You think Kitty Sue is your younger daughter?"

"That's the young woman I saw on Saturday?"

Anne nodded. "I was coming toward the ER and saw you watching her. Like you just had a revelation."

"I did, but then I had to figure out how to handle it without scaring the girls or getting them targeted. I didn't want anyone to know I was around, but there's no easy way to let them know about the heart condition they may have inherited."

"Katie's fine." Liam sounded almost defensive.

Anne put a hand of caution on his arm. "What is this condition?" she asked.

"The same thing that took their mother's life and their grandmother's before that. And their great-grandmother as well, although none of us ever put this together when Jeannine and I got married. We just thought it was an unfortunate coincidence." Kevin leaned against one of the tall supports framing the shaded area. "It's a congenital but sometimes undetectable defect that wasn't even really recognized twenty-five years ago. Jeannine's grandmother died in her late thirties. Her mother lived to her early forties, but we lost Jeannine a few days after Amelia was born. I inadvertently witnessed a mob hit, Jeannine gave birth to Amelia, and then she died, all in the same week. To say I was devastated is an understatement. And scared." His gaze shifted to the blanket of calm water.

"I was schooled in law and justice," he went on. "I'd witnessed a heinous crime against two people. I knew my testimony would change my life forever. And my family's lives. Then suddenly my wife was gone. My girls could become targets. But what kind of person would I be if I shrugged it all off and walked away, letting killers go free?"

Anne went straight to the altruism of the situation. "You made a supreme sacrifice."

"You make me sound noble. I was anything but." He drew a breath. "I hated everything then. For a while, anyway. Everything but my girls. All I wanted was for them to have a happy life, together." His attention shifted to Liam. "But that's not what happened, and I want to know why. Because in all the crazy that was swirling around me, I put them first, and there hasn't been a day that's gone by that I haven't questioned that decision. And now—"

It wasn't just his words that gripped Anne.

His expression grabbed hold too. As if his sacrifices had been wrong. All wrong.

"I'll find out what happened." The firm tone of Liam's voice offered confidence, but Kevin shrugged.

"What good will that do? It's done. My girls don't even know they're related."

Evelyn posed an obvious question. "How can you be sure that Kitty Sue is your daughter? Other than the obvious resemblance to Katie. That could be coincidence."

"They say everyone has a doppelgänger," added Joy.

Kevin pulled out his wallet. In the back, beneath a leather flap, he removed two pictures. One was a birthing suite picture of him holding an adorable, grinning toddler and a beautiful young woman holding a newborn swaddled in pink rose, a color that Kitty Sue favored to this day.

Then he handed them the second picture. Of his wife. She was at a beach, and she'd turned her head to smile for him and the camera, and there it was. The perfect image of Kitty Sue's face when she'd do that over-the-shoulder or sideways glance.

"I know we can run a DNA test," said Anne, "but that photo is proof enough for me. Kitty Sue is your late wife's mini-me."

"She sure is. But this all begs the question of who's been following Katie around?" asked Evelyn with typical practicality. "Is it you, Kevin? In a dark SUV?"

He refuted that swiftly. "I'm driving a Toyota Camry rental. I didn't want to drive my own car across country. I didn't intend to leave a trail when I set out," he reminded them. "My sole purpose was to make sure the girls get checked out. If they have the defect, it can be corrected. But if it isn't found, the sudden massive cardiac infarction comes unexpectedly and leaves little time for intervention."

"We'll make sure they both get checked," said Liam. "I promise. But if it's not you snooping around, who is it? And what do they want? That's another question in need of an answer. A quick one, because I don't want Katie hurt or scared."

"What happens if we test Kitty Sue's DNA and it comes back that Kevin's right?" Anne posed the question. "That Kitty Sue is the second daughter. She and her parents are totally out of the loop on all this, so they'd have to be brought up to speed. And by the way," she said to Kevin, "I've never met two nicer, sweeter, funnier, or smarter young women. They both have a great work ethic and beautiful faith. You should be very proud of the chance you gave them."

Consternation deepened the lines on his face. "I'm proud of them, yes. Even though I had nothing to do with it. I promised myself I would walk away completely, because nothing was more important than their safety and happiness, but I should have left a hole. An opening," he explained. "So that I could catch a glimpse from time to time. Enough to see they were all right. If I had, they never would have been separated."

"Even if it was for their own good?" Joy put the question out there. "Maybe it was done to remove one more obvious link."

"I made my expectations clear." Kevin gripped the back of a swing. "I left no doubt with the people handling the adoption. But there was no way to have them bury it as deeply as I wanted it buried and stick around to oversee things once I'd testified. Getting me out of Atlanta alive was a full-time job for one of the detectives on the case."

"Chas Murrow."

Kevin nodded to Liam. "Murrow oversaw everything. That guy kept me alive. To this day I'm grateful for his help."

"What do we do now?" Evelyn glanced at her watch. "We still need to find out who's watching Katie if it's not you."

"Oh, I'll keep an eye out." Kevin wasn't a burly man, but he had that lean strength of a man who kept himself in shape. "I didn't come east to save their lives only to have my questions raise red flags to mess them up."

"I'm not laying this at your doorstep." Liam squared his shoulders. "I don't know exactly what's going on, but unless the mob knows you're looking—"

"Which means a dirty cop, but I went through Murrow. No one else."

Liam's expression didn't change. Not really. But Anne caught the twitch of a tiny muscle just beneath his left eye.

Did he trust this other detective or not?

She couldn't tell, but she was pretty certain that Liam was going to find out what Murrow had to do with the girls' adoption, because if he was untrustworthy then, he'd be the last person they could trust now.

Chapter Nineteen

Charleston, South Carolina
Spring 1973

"Regina!" Susie spotted Regina as she cut across the street. Regina was carrying Miss Cynthia Ruth Bashore and hurried to meet her. "I can't believe you got over here in time to see us off." She wrapped her arms around Regina and hugged her, then stepped back. "I know how hectic you are at the hospital. And with the baby, besides. Oh, Regina, she is so cute. So sweet."

"Good as gold," declared Regina. "Little Miss Cynthia, can you give Miss Susie a kiss?"

The almost one-year-old leaned forward. She put two tiny hands up against Susie's cheeks and kissed her.

"Oh, that is so precious. What a sweet child you are. Regina, come on in. I'll put the kettle on, and we can—"

"We can do no such thing, because I know you're about to run out and get the last-minute things for your move. Thankfully Atlanta is full of stores so that anything you forgot is easily purchased. And you got a job right there in the heart of Forsyth County, Susie, teaching school. I hear that's a fine place to live."

Susie rolled her eyes. "Hollis is all over that, what with his promotion and all. He's had his share of city living and then some, he says, but I like the push and pull of people."

"It's always nice to get a pay raise and have a good place for Jeannine to go to school. And you know you're one to blossom wherever you're planted, my friend. It's your way."

But she understood Susie's lament.

Susie embraced the world.

Hollis embraced Hollis, and she didn't know what that would mean for the future, but for now it meant a pretty home on a shaded Southern street, away from the busyness of the city. "You call me if you're coming back this way, you hear? So we can get these children together to play. They'll be big enough for that, by and by."

"I will." Susie hugged her. "Same to you. If you head up Georgia way, come on by. I would love for you and Charles and Cynthia to come visit. That would make this move seem less absolute."

It did feel absolute. Regina wasn't sure why. Was it the difference in neighborhoods? Cities? The feeling of belonging they both felt in Charleston that might not be duplicated other places?

Cynthia squirmed with indignation.

"We're squashing her." Susie laughed and sprinkled butterfly kisses all over Cynthia's face. "Goodbye, Little Miss. Aunt Susie can't wait to see you again!"

"Have you got your picture?" asked Regina. They'd added a couple of new pictures over the last two years, both by the Angel of Mercy statue in full spring color. Susie had brought Jeannine over and they'd walked the waterfront, like always.

"Safe and sound in my personal moving box. Yours?"

"On the corkboard in my kitchen, so I can see it every single day. Call me, okay?"

"Oh, I will!"

They hugged one last time.

Regina wasn't sure Susie would call. Life got busy, people drifted apart, but whether she did or didn't, they'd shared a time that distance couldn't fade or erode.

They'd shared life.

Jeannine and Cynthia would be separated by years and miles, but the rise and fall of bringing these babies into the world was a chapter written in the stars. And stars hung together, even as life pushed them apart.

Because that was the way of stars.

Chapter Twenty

ANNE, SHIRLEY, AND JOY MET at the café the next morning. The early rush was over, but the dew hadn't dried on the outdoor tables and seating, so they took a table inside, far from the door.

Anne tugged her notebook out of her purse. "We drop in on Lee Spencer first?"

"We have to be careful there," advised Shirley. "We are all working at Mercy Hospital. If she's launched a lawsuit against the hospital, our visit could be seen as interference or an attempt to prejudice in the hospital's favor."

Joy turned, surprised. "You're right. I never thought of that." She made an "eek!" face at Anne. "Wilson had to lie low several times over the years when a simple conversation might have fixed things with people. Once the legal beagles are involved, anything you do can be used in the case or courtroom." She swung her attention back toward Shirley. "Did Garrison tell you that?"

"Don't think for a moment that I told that good man our plans." The dubious expression on Shirley's face made Anne and Joy laugh. "He's got enough on his mind handling this and that, but he did get a bit of nice information last evening that he said I could share. You know that active shooter alarm last week?"

As if anyone could forget. Joy and Anne leaned in to listen.

"Not sabotage." Shirley tapped a finger to the table. She kept her voice low. "Seamus tracked it down to a security programmer who was in the system the day before, changing code to foil hackers. He accidentally set a shooter drill in motion and then left for upper Pennsylvania because his mother is in hospice there. He was out of touch for several days. He felt awful when he realized what he'd done."

"That is so much better than the other option," breathed Joy. "The thought that someone had gotten into the system to do that deliberately was unnerving."

"Garrison seemed relieved," Shirley continued. "He was sweet to see me home, and he didn't just drop me off," she continued softly. "We took a nice walk around the neighborhood together."

"Oh, Shirley." Joy reached over and grasped Shirley's hand. "That's wonderful. It makes me smile. But on a practical note, I need our plan for today so I can text Sabrina that I won't be late to watch over my grand-girls."

"We might not be on solid ground to pay an actual visit to Lee Spencer." Shirley broke off another piece of the muffin. "But we could go 'round her way and check out what she drives. Where she lives."

"A scouting mission," said Anne.

"Just that," agreed Shirley.

"But how can we find out who had that SUV on Saturday?" wondered Joy. "That's a loose end I want tied up. Whoever was driving that van wanted us scared."

"A successful mission on his or her part," Anne assured her. "I was plenty scared. Then you and I went straight to mad. I like that about us."

Shirley swallowed her bite of muffin. "How do we find that person?" she asked.

Joy snapped her fingers. "We go back to the source. The owner of the courier service said he wanted to find out what happened. If I suggest possible legal action, that might loosen his tongue. Whoever was driving that big bruiser of a car needs to know that scaring people isn't taken lightly. If needed, I have the lawyers to follow through on it."

"I'm in." Anne wrapped up the second half of her muffin for later. "If we get a move on, we can all be home in a few hours. We're doing an early supper so Ralph can get to the hospital for the evening service tonight. He's doing a midday Good Friday service in the chapel tomorrow too." She tucked the muffin into a side pocket of her purse and stood. Joy and Shirley stood too. "They're streaming the services to the rooms," she told them, "so immobile patients can watch from the comfort of their beds. How cool is that?"

"Marvelous." Shirley led the way to the door. "I love when we use technology to reach people in need. Are you helping move patients downstairs again tomorrow, Anne?"

"Yes." When Joy began to compliment her, Anne waved a dismissive hand. "Only doing my job. This is just a nice side benefit toward helping folks feel a little bit of life's normalcy when their days are anything but normal. Ginger." She turned and waved to the auburn-haired café owner. "Tell Bud the muffins were marvelous. Like always."

"Will do!" Ginger waved a swipe cloth their way as she cleaned tables. "All y'all have a great day now, y'hear?"

"Sure thing, and the same to you."

They used Anne's car to check out Lee Spencer's neighborhood.

"Is it a coincidence that she's only about ten blocks from Gwyneth Lange's house?" wondered Joy as they did a slow, easy drive-by.

"Or that there's a black SUV in the driveway?" noted Shirley. "Could that be the one, ladies? Instead of the vehicle from the courier service's fleet?"

Anne shrugged. "No. The license plate points to the courier service."

Shirley shifted in her seat. She was riding shotgun. Joy sat directly behind her. "Joy?"

Joy looked out her window. "I only saw it for a couple of seconds. It was coming right at me, so I wasn't paying any attention to the details. I just wanted to get out of the way. But when it turned off at the last minute, I got a glimpse of the side windows." She pointed to the SUV in Lee Spencer's driveway. "That triangular back window seemed bigger. Longer. More like the one at the courier service."

"But then we could be dealing with more than a single SUV," noted Anne. "One that threatened us and another that followed Katie."

"If it was even following her." Shirley handed them each a printed photo. "I didn't want to talk about it in the café, but look at this. I got out a little before Garrison was done last evening, so I snapped a couple of pictures. These are the parking lots around six forty-five in the evening. Look at how many black or charcoal-gray SUVs there are in the lot." She'd taken a picture of the employee lot, the parking garage, and the adjacent harbor lots. "I counted thirty-two, and that's without actually going into the parking garage and up and down the levels."

Anne sighed. "So the one following Katie could have been random. Or someone else. Seamus said the plates were different from the one that scared us on Saturday, but also that they were mud-crusted, so he could only get a partial. Two numbers and a letter."

"It's illegal to drive with an obstructed plate," announced Joy. "But if I were going to do that, I'd use mud. Make it look as accidental as possible."

They pulled away from the Spencer house and headed north. It was a thirty-minute drive, but there were no awkward silences. Joy shared pictures of the cute dresses she'd gotten for her granddaughters. Anne had them pass around her phone and check out pics of Addie at her most recent horseback riding lessons and then told them the latest news. "Lili is letting her learn to jump."

"Wow—that's awesome." Shirley sounded delighted. "I love when parents encourage their little ones to be brave and bold. Good for Lili, Anne, although I'm not surprised, because anyone who makes it as a captain in the air force has to be pretty brave and bold herself."

"She's all that," agreed Anne. "And I'm proud of how well Addie's taken to riding and how good she's getting. To see her put a horse through its paces after less than a year's worth of lessons is amazing to me. Of course, I've never been on a horse, so the whole thing is a wonder. Here we are, ladies."

She drove around the back of the strip mall and parked. Two SUVs were parked there, but neither had the right plate number. They walked inside.

The same woman was behind the counter that separated her from the customers. When she recognized Anne and Joy, she lifted her brows. "You've returned."

"We need a follow-up," explained Joy. Her elongated drawl caused the words to feel less invasive, but she made her point clear. "I was hoping to hear from the manager—"

"Mr. Oswald is the owner. And the manager."

Joy acknowledged that with a slight frown. "So this is doubly troubling for him, having his business at stake. My husband owned several businesses in Houston, so I know this whole incident has put your boss into a tough position."

"He's a man of decision. The employee in question was relieved of his duties."

"The one who just had a baby?" The thought that their inquiry had cost someone his job raised Anne's concern. "He got fired?"

The woman seemed torn. "He didn't follow the rules. He broke the agreement. He didn't get the company car back here and left it accessible to others. That simply isn't done. It puts the owner and the company at risk, which then puts everyone's job on the line."

"So he's fired." Sincere sadness deepened Shirley's tone. "With a brand-new baby and a wife to care for."

The woman squirmed. "I know it's hard."

Anne hurried to assuage her. "Oh, this isn't your fault. I hope you don't think we're disapproving of you. Or of your rules. It's the circumstances, you know?"

The compassion in her voice loosened the woman's attitude. "And Robert was one of our best couriers. Always available, always took the calls, even at the worst possible times. Not all customers using our service are considerate of holidays or time of day. They want what they want when they want it. Of course, the cost to them skyrockets, but if they're rich enough not to care, then they get what they pay for. Robert never said no. In retrospect, that's what got him into trouble. The client wanted something done Friday night that should have been a quick turnaround, but when Robert got to the corporate offices, they weren't ready and kept him waiting for over ninety minutes."

"That's acceptable?" asked Shirley.

The woman shook her head. "No. The contract is for pickup and delivery upon courier arrival. It's not the courier's job to hang around while executives do whatever it is they do. Robert reported in and explained the problem, that he was caught there and his wife had gone into labor. Mr. Oswald was going to relieve him personally, but then the executive or whoever it was pulled it together and gave Robert the item to be delivered. And a tip."

"Couriers report tips?"

"He was quite honest with the boss about the whole thing when he came in on Monday."

"I thought he had paternity leave," said Joy.

"He does. He was called in specially."

"To be terminated."

The woman flushed. "Yes. I hate it because he was trying to do the right thing, but someone got ahold of the car and used it while he was at the hospital. He had no idea," she told them. "He'd parked it at Mercy Hospital's ER parking, and when he came out the next afternoon, it was still there. He never thought to check mileage."

"How could someone use the SUV without keys?" asked Shirley.

"He said he left the keys in the vehicle by mistake because the OB nurse called him. He said he didn't realize it until he came out on Saturday and the keys weren't in his jacket pocket. They were in the car. It's a keyless entry, so anyone could have taken the car in that space of time. The car won't lock if it senses the keys inside."

But why?

Why steal a car to scare them? Or was there another reason?

"Can you have Mr. Oswald give me a call, please?" Joy leaned over and handed the woman a slip of paper with her cell phone number on it. "And did the young couple have a boy or a girl?"

"A boy," said the woman. "They named him Benjamin. After Robert's grandfather."

Anne smiled. "Lovely."

They left, and no one dared say a word until they were back in Anne's car. There she recited the list of facts while Shirley jotted them down. "Mercy Hospital birth, early Saturday, baby's name is Benjamin and father is Robert."

"Robert Morgan," said Joy from the back seat. "I looked at the papers on her desk when I leaned over to give her the phone number. It was on a file folder, off to the side. My guess is that's our new father."

Shirley put the name into a search engine while Anne headed south toward the historic district. "He's twenty minutes from here," she announced a minute later. "Lives on Darlington Ave."

"The Wagener Terrace area," said Anne.

"Should we head over there?" asked Shirley.

"We're not far from it. Let's see what he has to say," agreed Joy. "Anne, is that all right?"

"We have a window of time and an actual address. So yes. Let's see what Robert Morgan can tell us."

Chapter Twenty-One

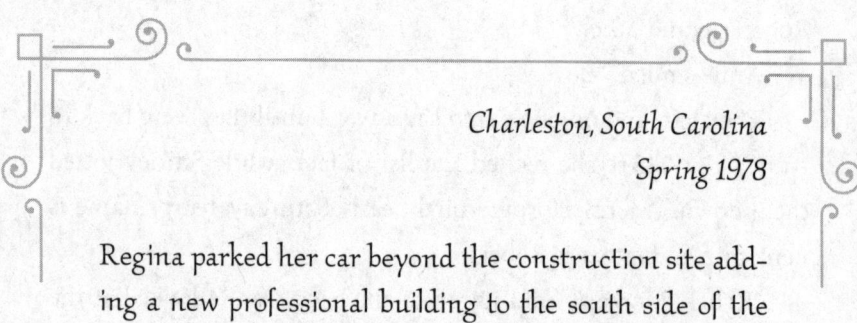

Charleston, South Carolina
Spring 1978

Regina parked her car beyond the construction site adding a new professional building to the south side of the hospital grounds.

Her mother used to say that change followed change, and it seemed to be the case here at Mercy. The face of the hospital was being expanded and updated all the time now. As advances in medical care progressed, so did Mercy. A huge endowment from the Gaylord Foundation had kicked off construction for a new hospital wing complete with surgical suites and a web-style ICU. The Gaylord family had thick, deep roots in South Carolina soil, particularly in Charleston. The younger Mrs. Gaylord insisted on delivering her children at Mercy because she preferred their homelike setting. Three babies later, the Foundation showed its gratitude with financial largesse. The new wing spurred other development, so the entire area had seen various kinds of construction for the past three years, with more scheduled, but that wasn't really on Regina's mind right now.

Today she was meeting Susie by the angel statue, and as she pushed six-month-old Shirley's stroller along the sidewalk, the spring air bathed her and the baby. They had just over two hours before Little Miss would be picked up from school. Not long enough for a true visit, but what they could spare from two busy lives. She turned the stroller up the walk and saw her friend right off. "Susie!"

"Regina!"

Susie ran her way, laughing. Always laughing. Just the sound of her friend's joy buoyed Regina's heart.

"You look marvelous!" exclaimed Susie. "And this baby, oh my goodness, Regina Bashore, I didn't think any cherub could be cuter than Little Miss, but this child is gorgeous! Those big brown eyes and all that hair? Hey, darling." Susie stayed back a few steps, perhaps so she wouldn't overwhelm Shirley, but the little girl took one look at the prattling stranger and burst into tears.

"It seems Aunt Susie has lost her touch, darling." Susie pretended a shocked face while Regina reached for the baby.

Regina snugged little Shirley into her shoulder, then rolled her eyes at Susie. "She has just this week gotten to recognize who she knows and who she doesn't know, so you're not the first to make her cry the past few days," she told her. "But we know how to fix this, my friend. You come behind the stroller with me, and we'll put Shirley back into her seat. She won't even know you're around."

"Subterfuge." Susie laughed, but she sounded like she wanted to cry. "Sounds good to me."

They began walking but paused at the statue. Susie reached out and took Regina's hand. Then she bent her head.

Susie was a pray-er. Talking to God was her go-to. She had a preacher's gift for heartfelt petition.

Today's prayer was silent.

Worry stirred Regina's gut. When Susie took her hand off the statue, she squeezed Regina's hand lightly. "It is good to be back here, my friend. Good to be home."

"What's going on, Susie?" They may have been hours apart for years, but Regina knew Susie well enough to know something was wrong. Really wrong. "Is everything all right?"

Susie's yes said one thing. Her expression said something else, and that fed the worry. "Is it Jeannine? Is she fine?"

"She's so good." Talking about Jeannine brightened Susie's gaze. "She's noble. I know that's an odd word to describe a child, but it's how I see her. She's always ready to fight for the underdog, and she studies, Regina! Oh, how she studies. It boggles my mind how smart she is, and she uses those smarts for good things. She's a Martha," Susie continued. "Reaching out for others all the time. Helping at school, helping at church, helping neighbors."

"A spirit that came direct from you and Miss Molly, Susie. You can take full credit on that." She didn't mean it as a slight to Hollis's pretentious nature, but it fit. "I can't wait to see her this summer when you all come down to visit Hollis's family."

"Except we won't be down here." The light in Susie's eyes faded again. "Hollis wants to host the family at our place."

Regina didn't hide her surprise. "Which means you'll be hosting the family." From their conversations and letters she knew that Hollis didn't see Susie's teaching job as essential, nor the tasks of motherhood and homemaking as things of importance, so thrusting a whole family visit on Susie might be a new twist, but it wasn't out of character. Hollis said jump and expected Susie to do so. The fact that she didn't was a growing bone of contention.

"The whole tribe is heading our way in July, and you know what that will be like. Heat and humidity galore and no pool. We've got a sprinkler, but if the grass gets muddy, Hollis gets upset, so don't ask me why we're doing this, because I have no answers. According to my husband, my task will be entertaining and feeding the entourage, because he doesn't dare take off work."

Hollis's family wasn't small. "All of them?"

Susie nodded. "I'm beside myself about it, not because I don't want them to come by, but to invite all of them to come and spend a week is crazy. He didn't tell me until a few days ago. I should be getting things ready for going back to school, but he brushed that off, even though I'm moving to the eighth-grade position in August and I have a lot of prep to do. When I tried to explain that to Hollis, he acted as if it didn't matter."

"As if you don't matter." Regina whispered the words, and her fears were confirmed when a tear slipped down Susie's cheek.

"He calls teaching 'my little job,' and he says it in that patronizing voice as if it's inconsequential. But nothing I do is inconsequential, Regina. And he needs to realize that."

"I saw that Hollis Stanton got another promotion. They mentioned it in the *Courier*, and it seems likely it went straight up, up, up to his noggin."

"It certainly did," replied Susie. "Those fancy titles he has after his name come with hefty salaries and lots of interesting opportunities for a man like my husband."

Regina drew her brows down, confused. Then the light dawned. "He's got himself a girlfriend?" The thought of anyone cheating on Susie still amazed Regina.

"His lack of satisfaction isn't limited to new advances in hospital machinery and health care. It seems to embrace life in general."

"Oh, Susie." Regina paused the stroller. They'd gotten down to the waterfront area, and a sweet breeze whispered through the shade-lined street. She reached out and hugged her friend. "Are you sure?"

"I am absolutely certain, and it's not his first walk outside the park. I know what I should do, Regina. I should walk away with my dear girl and start over. Remove her from him and his prideful ways, but she doesn't see that side of her daddy. Not yet, anyway, so which is the bigger sin? Me breaking up a family and wrenching her from her daddy, or him stepping out with someone new every six months or so?"

Regina knew what she would do, but she and Charles had a firm understanding of God's covenant of marriage from the get-go. And Regina wasn't one to tolerate nonsense.

Susie was different. More sensitive. And more dependent, even though there wasn't reason to be. "Girl, you could get by on your salary and child support, couldn't you?"

"He'd fight me, Regina. He'd get some high-priced lawyers, and you know they'd drag me through the mud. Hollis wouldn't be caring about Jeannine's feelings in all this. He'd care about winning. And there are plenty of judges in Forsyth County that would take his side. A good Southern gal doesn't just up and leave a hardworking husband as long as he's not going to jail. More's the pity we haven't made carousing a felony."

Hollis was just in it for the show.

She'd sensed it long ago but hoped it wasn't the case. Susie's confession said otherwise. "Oh, Susie." She hugged her friend's arm. "Honey, I'm so sorry. So sorry."

"I know. If I do leave at some point, I'll come back here. Teach here. For me this is home, and I think it always will be."

There was little to say, because Regina couldn't make this better. She sighed. "We fix what we can, my friend. But marriage is different, Susie. Will he go to counseling?"

"Hollis?" Susie raised both eyebrows.

Regina sighed. "I knew the answer before I asked the question. I will take this to prayer. Every single day I will ask God to give you strength."

"And courage."

"Oh, you have that, Susie. It's just been on a shelf awhile. All it needs is a dusting off."

Susie smiled and hugged Regina's arm. "This is why we're so close. You believe in me. I believe in you. We love one another because we're friends on a well-traveled road."

"Like that band of women who followed the cross up Calvary, we stay true."

Susie smiled in agreement, wiped her eyes with a tissue, then pointed. "And that new ice cream place is calling our name. We have just enough time to get one and enjoy it before I have to hit the road."

She'd changed the subject on purpose, and Regina let it go. They'd said enough. Talking it to death wouldn't help.

Susie got a vanilla cone dipped in chopped pecans.

Regina got a dish of black raspberry custard, her favorite, so she could share it with the baby. They found a bench facing the water. Before them the harbor stretched toward the North Atlantic. The water lay in quiet magnificence today. Tiny waves lapped the shore, but that wasn't always the case. Like folks, the ocean could change its face mighty quick, and Regina had lived through enough storms to know tempests would run their course eventually and the sea would calm.

Then another storm would come.

It was the time in between she appreciated, the time of peace and normalcy. But as she sat there with Susie, it seemed like her friend's normal might never be at peace again, and that realization hurt her heart.

Chapter Twenty-Two

"WE CAN'T GO THERE WITHOUT a gift," said Shirley as they neared a strip mall on the way to Robert Morgan's house. "This family has been through enough and through no fault of their own, near as I can tell. Let's get them a grocery gift card. Diapers are expensive."

"I'm in." Anne parked the car outside the store and slipped a fifty out of the back of her wallet. "This is my goodwill money. This is the perfect way and the perfect week to put it to use."

"I'll call," declared Joy as if she'd just been dealt a great hand in a round of poker. She slipped two twenties and a ten up to Shirley. "Wilson loved Texas Hold'em, and I'm pretty good if I say so myself."

"I'll add mine inside," said Shirley. She dashed in, and when she came back out, she tucked a gift card into the console between the front seats. "Now I'll feel better checking this whole thing out," she announced as she snapped her shoulder belt into place.

"When the Holy Spirit puts a need in front of us—"

"We'd be wrong to ignore it, and having a baby should come with no extra worries," Shirley finished for Anne.

They pulled up in front of a brick bungalow on Darlington Avenue about fifteen minutes later.

"Is it too many if we all go to the door?" wondered Joy, just as a man emerged from the house. He came their way. He wasn't the twentysomething young man Anne expected. This fellow had a few extra decades packed on.

Anne got out of the car. Shirley and Joy did the same.

"Mr. Morgan?" she asked.

"That's me. One of them, anyway."

"Did you work for Charleston Couriers?" Anne continued.

He shook his head. "That's my son. Robert. Is this about him getting fired? Because that was a rough deal."

"It's about the SUV." Joy moved a little closer. "I was driving the car that was threatened by that SUV Saturday morning."

"You all right?" He had the kindness to look concerned. "Those are big vehicles."

"Fine, sir. Thank you for asking," Joy replied. "Is Robert here? Or do we have the wrong house?"

"He's here. He was just handing little Ben over to his mother for a midday snack. We haven't had a newborn around in a lot of years, so my wife and I are six shades of happy, let me tell you. Except for the job thing." He frowned, worried. "That's a kick in the head for a man who's worked hard. Let me give Rob a heads-up." He pulled out a cell phone and texted his son. A moment later, a handsome young man came through the side door and crossed the short driveway to meet them.

"First, this is for you," announced Shirley. She handed the gift card to him. "Use it for whatever you need for that new baby. We were sorry to hear that you were let go following our visit to Charleston Couriers," she added, then indicated Joy with a nod. "My friend here was the one involved in that near accident on Saturday morning."

"I'm the one who lodged the complaint," admitted Joy. "But I didn't mean to get you fired, and I'm just sick about it with all you've got going on."

The younger man didn't take the card or accept her guilt. "It was my fault," he said firmly. "I know the rules." He met her concern with a level gaze. "There were extenuating circumstances, but I should have made sure I put the keys in my jacket pocket like I always do. I got a call from a nurse at the Arabella Center just as I pulled into the parking area, and I hit the ground running. Once Ben was born, everything else went out of my head. It was irresponsible. And when you're working for other people, that's not a choice."

"It was a mistake, pure and simple," Anne told him. "And you'll make us feel badly if you don't take the card, young man, and you wouldn't want to make three nice ladies feel bad during Holy Week, would you?"

Her prodding relaxed his expression. "I would hate to do that."

"Good." Joy smiled up at him as Shirley handed over the gift. And he smiled back.

"But who would have stolen that SUV and then returned it?" wondered Anne out loud. "That's the question. It doesn't make sense that some random person happened to stroll by, notice the unlocked vehicle, target us, then put it back. The entire scenario defies logic."

"I've gone up one side of it and down the other," replied Robert. "I was delayed at Miles & Miles, Inc. They had a rush file to get to Alistair, Bausch & Bausch but had some last-minute changes after the stock market closed. I was about to leave when they handed the file to me. My boss had called and told them that I was leaving and why and that he'd come over, but that he wasn't about to hurry. He figured their lack of concern about my time should be repaid in kind. He wasn't pleased they held me up. His call got things moving. They handed me the courier pouch, I drove to A, B & B, and a friend of mine met me inside. He's a lawyer like his dad, only he does corporate stuff. Anyway, they were about to go out to supper and had to put the brakes on because I showed up, but I didn't have time to chitchat. Fortunately, their office is on Tradd and only a block from the hospital. I dropped the package off and drove straight over to the birthing center."

"Is there really stuff that has to get handled on a Friday night when we're all dragging?" asked Shirley. "I mean other than life or death?"

"I guess," answered Robert Jr. "If that's your thing. Ryan—that's my friend—he and his brother are sons of the second Bausch, so when your father's a partner, you put in the overtime, I guess. Their dad was always climbing the ladders of success, and Ryan and George are like that too. Me?" He shrugged. "I want a job that pays decent and gives me time with my family. In three months I'll have my secondary school teaching certification, and I won't be running courier pouches anymore."

"Teaching is a great profession," said Anne.

Robert slung an arm around his father. "My dad's been teaching for thirty-six years. My mom too. They met on their first assignment. They taught me and my brothers to love words and numbers and thoughts. I was programmed to love learning." He gave his dad a half hug, and the expression of love when he looked at his father was sweet. Really sweet. "It'll be nice to walk into a classroom on the other side of the desk in August."

"He's already gotten a job at Lincoln Academy," bragged his father. "So all we've got is a few months to get through, and we're set enough to handle that."

"Congratulations. That part makes us happy," said Joy. "But I'm still bummed about the lost job thing. You said you went from one company to another for the courier pouch?" she asked.

"Law firms," he said. "It's usually contract stuff. Final negotiations. And they're always in a hurry. Except for this last time."

"Isn't that the way of it?" Shirley said. "Robert, thank you for talking to us. And congratulations on your new baby."

"I'm just glad no one was hurt," he said. "That would be a very different conversation, and I'm glad we're all spared that."

"We are too." Anne reached out and shook both men's hands. "Have a blessed Easter. All of you."

Robert Senior smiled at her. "You too."

The women got back into the car.

Anne tapped the steering wheel. She met Joy's eyes through the rearview mirror. "I believe him."

"Me too," replied Joy.

"But we don't buy into coincidences."

"Not generally." Shirley puffed out a breath as Anne started the engine. "Although every now and again they happen. We can't discount that as a possibility."

Anne shook her head. Then she paused. "I did park my car in the usual spot," she said thoughtfully.

"I picked you up there and dropped you off there." Joy stretched forward in her seat. "Do you think someone deliberately followed us to Gwyneth's house?"

"But who?" asked Anne. She wasn't expecting an answer. "Could it be Liam or Kevin? They both knew we were looking into things. Liam because he asked us to, and Kevin because he's been watching."

"They both had proximity," noted Shirley.

"Kevin said he rented a car so he couldn't be traced," added Joy. "I expect when you're in witness protection you're schooled in ways to hide in plain sight."

"That would mean Kevin's interest in finding his daughters isn't sincere." Anne drew her brows together as she headed back toward the lower peninsula. "And I believe him. I *want* to believe him," she added. "So maybe that's coloring my judgment."

"Then it's coloring mine the same way," said Joy as they drew closer to her house, "but at this moment, those two supposed family men are at the top of the suspect list, and they're not in first and second place. They're running neck and neck, and it's anyone's guess who turns out to be the bad guy."

Anne didn't want it to be either man, but the few facts they had surrounded Mercy Hospital, and that brought them right back to the two men who had a twisted path that linked them to two young nurses.

But which man truly had the women's best interests at heart?

That was a question she couldn't answer. And—

Her musings were interrupted when Shirley's phone pinged an incoming text. She raised the phone up for Joy to see and read the message out loud. "Katie says she has another mystery solved!"

"What does she mean?" asked Anne. She was busy navigating through three lanes of traffic and didn't dare sneak a peek.

"Her plant," announced Shirley. "Not stolen. Her neighbor saw it suffering and took it for some clandestine CPR. She didn't want to insult Katie but couldn't bear to see a beautiful braided ficus fade away. The ficus is back home now, looking healthier and happier. With instructions attached!"

"Now that sounds like something I would do," said Joy. "It's amazing how a little pinching and pruning can set things right."

"It's the knowing what to pinch and prune that you and Mama have in common," said Shirley. She texted Katie back and tucked the phone away. "So now we have the answer to that. Good."

"I like that we can take that concern out of the picture," agreed Anne as she made a smooth left turn toward the harbor. "That leaves us more time to figure out which man means harm to Katie. Kevin? Or Liam? That's just become the question of the hour."

Chapter Twenty-Three

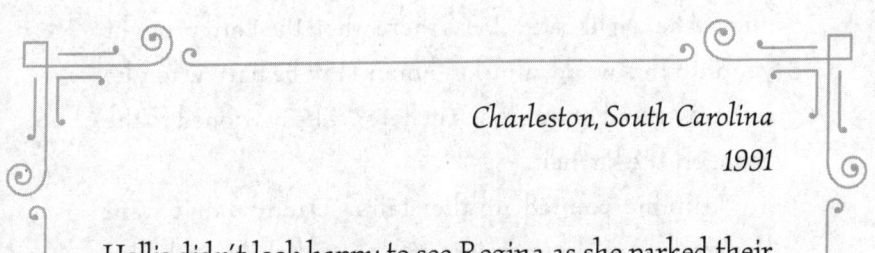

Charleston, South Carolina
1991

Hollis didn't look happy to see Regina as she parked their new station wagon in the Stanton driveway.

She tamped down her negative reaction because today wasn't about Hollis. It was all about Susie.

And saying goodbye.

Her heart clenched at the thought, and she had to bite back the rise of emotion. Time enough for crying and sobbing on the drive south. For now, she'd put on a brave face for a brave friend whose heart was giving out. She walked up the nicely edged sidewalk. "How are you, Hollis? I'm so sorry for what all y'all are going through."

"She called you?"

So much for pleasantries. "Yes."

He clammed up then, as if she wasn't worth talking to. He picked up a hose and began watering a lawn that didn't need watering.

Regina walked up the steps, tapped on the door, and walked inside.

"I'm so glad you're here!" Jeannine spotted her from the stairs. "Mama will be thrilled to see you, Miss Regina. She's been asking. I kept telling her you were on your way, and she would smile and nod, then ask again."

"Oh, honey." Regina hugged Jeannine, and Jeannine hugged her right back. "I was there when the Lord brought you into this world, and I'm honored to be here when he calls my friend home. Is she in here?" She motioned to the room off the kitchen.

Jeannine pointed up the stairs. "Daddy didn't want the confusion downstairs, and he said she'd be better off up there where nothing bothers her, which means he didn't want the bother of having a sick wife downstairs. But you know Daddy."

"I surely do, child." Regina slipped off her shoes and padded up the stairs behind Jeannine.

"Charles must have his hands full looking after the girls," Jeannine said.

"Yes, he took a couple of days off so I could be here with your mama."

"Good for him. And how's Little Miss liking the university?"

"Oh, I haven't heard Cynthia called Little Miss in a while, and it brings back such good memories. Your mama and I had such a fun time having you babies, caring for you, raising you. Even when we were far apart we'd call or write. It meant something, you know?"

"It sure did." Susie added those three words in a small voice. Regina headed to one side of the bed while Jeannine flanked the other. "Sweet saints, I'm that glad to see you, my friend. Although our visit will be short."

"Then you can save a spot for me with the angels, by and by." Regina gripped Susie's hand lightly. "Doesn't matter who goes first, it's just a matter of keepin' my rockin' chair oiled and ready."

Susie smiled. Then she grimaced, and Regina addressed Jeannine. "Do we have pain meds, pretty girl?"

"She wouldn't take them, because she wanted to be awake to see you."

"Mission accomplished," declared Regina. "But suffering through pain for no purpose is a kind but silly choice, so, Susie Stanton, I want you to take your meds and let me know if you need more, all right? Is there a visiting nurse that comes by?"

"Every day," Jeannine answered. "Mama said I should get back to work, but a one-hour visit from the nurse isn't enough. I told her in no uncertain terms that she stood by me during those touch-and-go first weeks, and I intend to return the favor. The hospital knows what I'm doing, and if they have a problem with it, there are other places to work. Mama comes first."

"I can't believe I'm talking to a full-fledged registered nurse." Regina smiled at Jeannine while Susie took the pills, then she winked at Susie's accomplished daughter. "You've done us proud, Jeannine."

"Thank you, Miss Regina."

Jeannine had set a kitchen chair alongside the bed on Regina's side. It was retro-style with padding and vinyl covering, but the air-conditioning kept the vinyl cool. Regina took a seat. "Now, if there is anything you need, my friend, you tell me," she told Susie. "Consider me your night nurse, all right? Just like the old days."

"Regina, are you sure?"

"100 percent."

"I'm so glad you're here, Miss Regina," Jeannine said, dashing away a tear. "I can't sleep at night, thinking of Mama being alone. I've been staying here. Right here."

Susie gestured to a narrow, upholstered chair. A small pillow sat on the seat and a hand-crocheted throw was slung across the back, indicating where Jeannine had slept the last few days.

"She won't be alone now, sugar."

Regina's promise eased Jeannine's shoulders. "I'm so glad. We've missed you all so much."

"Same here. Now, I brought a little fancy work to keep my hands busy while we sit and have a chat or watch our gal sleep. Either way is fine with me." She aimed a look at Susie's beautiful daughter and hoped she'd hear what Regina couldn't say. "Why don't you go catch a nap? Or at least a little break? I'll call you right quick if needs be."

Susie whispered agreement. "I told her that very thing," she said, but when she spoke, there was a pause between each word as air evaded her. "But she has sat right here, blessed child that she is."

Jeannine understood Regina's silent message, that two old friends might have things to say. Things that shouldn't be overheard.

She stood, bent and kissed her mother's cheek, then brushed her pretty eyelashes against her mother's papery skin. "Butterfly kisses, for you, Mama. Just like always. And whenever I see a butterfly coming by, acting all sweet and floaty, I'll know you're with Him and doing fine. So fine."

"I'll be watching," Susie promised.

"Didn't expect anything less, Mama." Jeannine stood. She swiped her hands to her cheeks as she left and when she half closed the door, Regina dabbed the tears from Susie's eyes.

"Now how are you going to say what needs to be said if you're carryin' on? You know that medicine is going to take hold soon and drift you into slumberland."

"And each time it does, I wonder if it will be the last time I waken on this side of that mountain," Susie said. "I didn't take the pills," she continued. "They work quick, and there's things that need saying. I need to have someone know what I know. Someone to look after my precious girl, because you know her daddy will be busy."

Regina understood. Hollis was a very busy man.

"Dear friend, you know I will." Regina squeezed Susie's hand gently. "But here's the truth, Susie. You've gone and raised yourself a fine young woman. A professional. And things are different for us now. Women are taking hold of their lives. They're standing up for themselves, and you raised this girl right. She pushed her way through nursing school, and she'll do the same with life. There isn't a soul that's going to take advantage of her, I promise you that." She leaned in and kissed Susie's cheek. The faint blue coloring of Susie's lips and fingernails marked the urgency of timing. "But I'll watch. I surely will. Same as I did when she was born. We stand strong and we stand together, and a heavenly address for you won't change that. And now, take those pills."

Susie's eyes filled with relief. She let Regina help her with the pills and the water. She sank back into the pillow, and her fair hair haloed her worn face. As she drifted to sleep, her face relaxed. Slumber eased the wear-and-tear look of terminal illness, and when Jeannine slipped back into the room a half hour later, she paused. "She looks like an angel, doesn't she, Miss Regina? With her hair splayed out like that, all soft around her head? And her face." Jeannine sank into the chair she'd placed on the opposite side of the bed. "So calm. So peaceful. That's all you, you know." She aimed a look of appreciation at Regina. "She knew you'd come. She said 'I know I'll relax once Regina's here, honey. Regina knows how to look after things.'"

And she did.

For the next three days she put her faith and nursing skills to work, and when she and Jeannine sent their beloved Susie home to God, it was with great sadness but no regret, because they'd shown their love all along. And that meant everything.

Chapter Twenty-Four

A BROKEN RELAY TO THE red elevators made the Good Friday service run late. That meant bringing patients down and then back up with fewer open cars and a delay all around. But Ralph gave a beautiful, heartfelt service, and more than one tear was shed as a small group from the St. Michael's choir offered a soul-stirring rendition of "Were You There?" to finish the prayerful liturgy.

Anne wasn't worried about the time. They were having two friends from St. Michael's and Lili and Addie for a fish supper, but there was plenty of time to get things ready as long as traffic didn't snarl the roads. But first, a different stop, one she made every Easter season.

She grabbed her purse and started across the lobby toward the ER entrance. Slipping out there would save her walking an extra half block outside, although the day was nice. Muggy but nice.

She crossed the parking lots, jaywalked across the street because it was fairly quiet, and hurried to her car.

She rarely went straight home on Good Friday, unless the weather was awful. It wasn't awful today. A perfect day to stop at Ariane's gravesite. She'd gotten a colorful bouquet of flowers from Joy. She settled them into the back seat and drove across the river to the tree-lined cemetery.

Ralph would have come if she'd asked. She knew that. But every now and then she wanted to have a girl-day with her precious daughter, gone too soon. A moment to sit. To think. Remember and pray.

She wasn't angry. Not anymore.

She was at first. The anger had curled up inside her. Some days it threatened to choke her, and she'd shove it back because she couldn't let it take hold. She couldn't let it own her. She was a minister's wife, a woman of faith, and she had a baby to care for.

Pushing the pain aside had been a mistake, because it did take hold. For too long, she thought now, although then it seemed like too short a time. And it felt wrong, maybe even more grievous, to be able to laugh again, enjoy Lili's exuberant personality, and be held in her husband's arms.

She'd seen for herself that grief and guilt made a noxious twosome. Now when she came to the shady cemetery, it was to remember the golden-haired little girl who spoke at such a young age, as if she had so much to tell them and not enough time to say it. Ralph used to enjoy that about her, the way she chattered about everything and anything.

Prophetic words.

She parked the car beneath the live oaks lining the roadway. Others had come today too. A somber day for thoughtful remembrances. As she crossed toward Ariane's plot, a familiar person stood in her path, just to the upper left of Ariane's grave.

Lee Spencer.

Anne paused.

Should she go on? Sidle past? Slip away? Would the woman even recognize her?

Maybe not. She walked along the pathway between the rows and followed it up to her daughter's grave. They'd gotten a big headstone. Not huge, but large enough to have their names inscribed too. Ariane's name was carved into the far left. The image of a lamb in a garden offered mute testimony to her young age. To the right were Ralph's and Anne's names. Not because she thought it was good to prepare, but the stone carver was already working on the stone, so she got it done.

She bent over and tucked the flowers into the vase at the foot of the gravestone.

She knew where Ariane was. Right back where she came from, a child of God. But standing there wondering what Ariane would be like as an adult always put a crimp in her emotions.

She sat down. They'd put a bench alongside, with a stone seat, just wide enough for two people to sit. To pray. And think. After a moment she looked up and saw Lee Spencer staring at her. Then the grave. Then her again.

Anne met her gaze. She dipped her chin slightly, and Lee's face crumpled.

Her hands shook. She clenched them together, but the effort proved fruitless. The shaking continued.

Anne stood and crossed the short span of graves. "How can I help?"

"You can't." A sob ripped from the woman's throat. Her neck convulsed, and Anne did what she would do for anyone in such a state. She wrapped her arms around Lee and let her cry.

Supper didn't matter. Supper could be late. What mattered was here, now, the utter breakdown of grief. She held the woman until the sobs lessened then pulled back. "Come sit with me. Please. I have tissues."

She led Lee back to the bench. They sat. She handed off a clutch of tissues and prayed silently while Lee worked to compose herself. And when the grieving woman finally leaned against the bench and took a deep breath, Anne spoke. "I hated coming here at first."

"Your daughter?" Lee jutted her chin toward the classic gray and ivory stone. "I'm so sorry."

"Leukemia. They tried everything," Anne said softly. "Ariane was treated by several hospitals, but in the end, the cancer was smarter than the science, and she went home to Jesus. I was so angry."

Lee dabbed her eyes again. "I know. And I hate being like this, because it's not good for me. For my kids. For anyone. I'm a wreck, and I want to punch God because He knew better. He knows me. Understands me. He knew better than to snatch my husband away like that, and then He let me down at the last minute. I've been mad. So very mad," she went on. "I want someone to pay. To make it right. To fix it."

She drew a deep breath, then turned toward Anne. "There is no fixing it now, because he's gone. And I can never say the things I needed to say. I can never fix that the last words between us were a stupid argument over updating the bathroom. He wanted to wait. I wanted it done before the holidays, as if the Lord's birthday was dependent on me having new shower tile. He wanted to wait until spring and get our daughter's tuition paid off." She turned to Anne more fully. "I wanted the bathroom done to show Sally that we were doing fine financially. She's my worrier. She internalizes everything, and if she thought we were putting things off in order to help pay for college, she'd get anxious and guilt-ridden. Her sister's the total opposite."

Anne appreciated the frank note in Lee's voice.

"Martha would just shrug that off as no big deal, but not Sally. She was like her dad that way, and maybe if I'd explained it to him, we wouldn't have fought over it. But we did, and halfway through the day, he was gone. Just like that." She went quiet. Her mouth opened slightly, and she sat there like that for a few moments before shaking herself. "I tried to get to the hospital. I told them to keep him alive, I was only minutes away."

Her chin quivered again. She firmed it and dabbed at her eyes. "But traffic was snarled two exits up, and by the time I got to Mercy, he was gone. Just—" She gripped the tissues, drew a breath, and sighed. "Gone. That young nurse told me what happened, that they tried to do everything they could, but despite their best efforts…" She sighed again.

She didn't have to repeat the oft-heard words. Anne knew them by heart. "I'm so sorry for your loss." She reached out and touched Lee's hand. "Words unspoken. Work unfinished. Death is so inconvenient. We assume life will go on, and when it doesn't, we're surprised. Of course, that's silly on our part, because God's word says that no one knows their time, but we live in a world of expectations. Did your husband love you?"

Lee drew back, startled, then nodded. "Yes."

"And you loved him."

"Yes."

"Do you think that quarrel was anywhere near his thoughts when he realized he was going home to God?" asked Anne softly.

"Well—"

Anne shook her head. "You know it wasn't. You know he was probably wishing the same thing you were, that he could have one last chance to say he was sorry, that he wanted the bathroom to be beautiful and your children to have happy lives. And that he would miss you. A silly argument would be the last thing on his mind."

"You think so? Really?"

"I do." Anne offered gentle reassurance like she'd done with parishioners for many years when she and Ralph served St. Michael's. "We all speak words in anger. We all have remorse. We all have regrets. But God has given you a mandate, hasn't He? To comfort your girls, to help them out, to take care of things the best you can. That's so much easier to do when we shake off the anger and move forward. Guilt and grief are a powerful pair. They'll own us if we let them. But we can't let them, because 'we have promises to keep. And miles to go before we sleep…'" She let the Robert Frost quote dangle, and Lee took another breath—a longer one—and looked up into Anne's eyes.

"And miles to go before we sleep."

Anne smiled and stood.

So did Lee. She swiped her sleeve across her face again. "I'm sorry I interrupted your time with her." She indicated Ariane's grave with a look.

"You didn't. You gave me an opportunity to be the kind of person my little girl would want me to be," Anne assured her. "The kind of person she would have been if she hadn't been called home so soon."

Lee tugged the strap of her small messenger bag higher on her shoulder. "Thank you."

Anne shook her head. "No thanks needed. You heading out?"

"In a bit." Lee turned toward her husband's grave. "I think I'll sit a while. Just to see."

"I understand. I'm Anne, by the way. Anne Mabry."

"Lee Spencer."

Anne didn't say she knew that already. The last thing this woman needed was to realize her antics were known around the hospital. She started down the pathway.

"Anne?"

Anne turned and looked back.

"I'll call my lawyers off."

Anne shifted an eyebrow up in question.

"For the lawsuit. I'll tell them to leave it alone. They won't necessarily like it, but they'll do it."

Garrison would be thrilled to have the shadow of a malpractice suit lifted. "Thank you, Lee. That would be nice. Have a blessed Easter."

"I'll try." She said it, and Anne was pretty sure she meant it as much as she could right now. Then she amended it slightly. "I mean I will. We will."

Anne walked back to her car. The live oaks hung full and heavy along the driving lanes, creating a majestic Southern feel. She texted the crew when she got back to the car. JUST HAD A HEART-TO-HEART WITH LEE SPENCER. SHE'S NOT THE ONE. NARROW YOUR LISTS ACCORDINGLY. AND, EASTER BONUS: SHE'S NOT GOING TO SUE THE HOSPITAL. SO THAT'S WONDERFUL NEWS.

She didn't say that her discovery left Liam and Kevin as prime suspects in her book. Liam was on the text, and she didn't want him to know he was a suspect. Kevin already knew he was a suspect, but maybe Liam was right. Maybe it was the mob, seeking revenge.

But who were they, where were they, and how did they remain so hidden? And how did they get their hands on the courier's SUV?

It made no sense.

None. So maybe it wasn't the mob after all.

Anne's thoughts swirled all evening long, until they were sitting around after dinner, chatting about this, that, and the other thing, the way friends do.

"Dad, you know how it is." Lili was curled up on the couch, chatting with her father and Thomas Dupont, an old family friend. Ralph had just waved a check for two dollars and fifty cents for everyone to see, their portion of a monster-sized class-action suit lawyers had brought against a marketing company several years before.

Lili shifted one eyebrow up at the miniscule amount of a multimillion-dollar award. "In the end, the only ones who win are the lawyers."

Ralph and Thomas laughed in agreement.

Anne didn't laugh.

She was rinsing plates in the kitchen when the words hit the light bulb switch in her brain.

Lawyers.

Those adoptions had lawyers involved. Hadn't Liam assured them at the beginning that Katie's adoption was totally legal?

Clean dishes could wait. She turned the water off and hurried to her laptop on the breakfast island. She put in the names Robert Morgan had given them.

Two major law firms came up.

Then she punched in the names individually and found that Philip Bausch had worked in Atlanta prior to moving to Charleston twenty-four years ago.

On a hunch she called Liam directly. "I have a quick question for you."

It was an obvious conundrum now, and she felt a little silly for not seeing the possibility before.

"Okay," Liam responded. "What's on your mind?"

"Who was the lawyer that arranged or oversaw the girls' adoptions? Well, Katie's, at least. You wouldn't have access to Kitty Sue's information."

"I'll call Sunny and get right back to you." He did too. Within a minute he had a name. A very familiar and now local name. "Phil Bausch. He handled it on the Atlanta end. He was a friend of one of the detectives on the case."

"An adoption attorney?"

"I don't know, actually," Liam replied. "On Sunny's end, yes. They used an adoption attorney. All I know is that after paying a lot of out-of-pocket expenses for fertility treatments that didn't work, she told me they spent a cool sixty grand to cover the adoption costs. Their lawyer's fee was eighty-two hundred. The rest went to the Atlanta firm." A thick pause added emotion to his next words. His voice deepened. "They *sold* those babies."

"I think so," replied Anne. "Fifty grand for an adoption would spark interest. That is, if someone's looking."

"And Kevin Eddington started looking." Liam took a deep breath. "I'll get ahold of him, but, Anne, I think you could be right. The lawyer and the detective might have been in this together. Chas

Murrow wasn't just a good detective. He was great. Smart enough to have hidden something like this away. And if he was willing to sell two little girls for profit, he might be willing to do a whole lot more to protect his very lucrative pension and reputation."

A shiver chased down Anne's spine, but disgust sent it on its way. "You check things out on your end. Let's get together tomorrow morning to fill the others in. You call Kevin. I'll send a group text to the rest and see who's available. All right?"

"Yes, absolutely. And Anne?"

"Yes?"

"Good job."

She breathed a sigh of relief because it was a job well done, but she knew one thing. The job wasn't over yet.

Chapter Twenty-Five

Charleston, South Carolina
1995

"She's here, Miss Regina! Miss Emily Eddington, seven pounds, one ounce, about twenty inches long from stem to stern, with her daddy's eyes and my flair for fashion!"

Regina laughed. "Jeannine, I've been praying nonstop ever since you went into labor, darling. Oh, what good news this is. Marvelous news! I loved getting up there with the girls for the baby shower, but I can't wait to see this pretty gal in person. Congratulations!"

"We'll be down this summer at some point for a quick visit. You'll love her, Miss Regina. My only regret is that Mama doesn't get to meet her. Hold her. Talk to her about all the beauty of the earth."

"You'll do all that for her, I expect," Regina said, wiping a tear from her eye.

"I sure will, Miss Regina." Jeannine sighed, a sigh of absolute and complete happiness. A sound of joy. "I think you're right. We'll see you this summer."

Jeannine came whirling into town mid-June, and oh! Didn't she just look like the young professional woman she was? Her pretty hair pulled up in a bun, her infant wrapped in some kind of sling across her chest, and every inch of her figure back in shape. "Look at you, girl! And Jeannine!" Regina hugged Susie's daughter gently and beamed at the baby. "Now, where is Kevin?"

"He's doing double duty on this trip," Jeannine drawled. "Greeting family in the nicest way and working on some research for a friend of a client. It's not his favorite job, mostly because it's not a favored client, but he's living up to his end of the bargain. My daddy may have been a slug, but my husband says what he means and means what he says."

"How much time do we have?"

"Time enough for ice-cold tea, a spot of nursing, and a diaper change. Wait." Jeannine paused when Cynthia came out the door. "Little Miss! Look at you being prettier than a hothouse orchid on Easter morning. Girl, you're gorgeous!" Jeannine had unfastened baby Emily from her sling. She handed her over to Regina and slung an arm around Cynthia's shoulders. "We're grown up now. Isn't it weird? I keep waiting for someone older and smarter than me to make the decisions that need making, and then I realize that it's a game of tag and I'm 'it.' How are you, Cynthia?"

"I'm engaged."

Jeannine put on a shocked face and swung back toward Regina. "Way to bury the lede! Why didn't you tell me?"

"Not my announcement to tell," Regina replied, and instantly felt bad about fudging the truth. That wasn't the reason she hadn't mentioned Cynthia's engagement. She'd kept it quiet because she didn't like Malcom Terhune, even if he had been one of the best quarterbacks the USC Gamecocks had ever known. He'd won Cynthia's heart during their senior year, and when Cynthia Bashore set her mind to something, there was no changing it. That meant a wedding—which should be a wonderful thing—and her girl would be leaving, going all the way to California, because that was what Malcolm wanted. He didn't pay any mind to Cynthia's family, no sir. He demanded to be close to his family, and what Malcolm desired, he got. The very thought sent mental red flags waving, but no one asked for Regina's opinion.

It worried her that her very smart daughter hadn't stood her ground. It made the whole deal sound way too much like Susie and Hollis back in the day. But grown children were grown, and she had to respect her child's choices, even when it was hard.

"When's the wedding?" asked Jeannine.

"October," Cynthia told her. "When things cool off. We don't want a big wedding."

That was Cynthia's practicality talking.

"But when we resettle in California, Malcolm's parents are going to throw us a party. That way folks don't have to spend money traipsing across the country. The last thing I want to do is cost Mama and Daddy more money. They helped with college. That was enough."

"You're a wise owl, Little Miss."

Jeannine's words put a light in Cynthia's eyes. She laughed, and it felt good to hear the fullness of her laughter. "He's a keeper, Jeannine. Like your Kevin."

Regina held her tongue, because maybe he would be. Maybe he was just young and full of himself. Maybe he would settle into married life and work the way a good man should. She sincerely hoped that would be the case.

Shirley pulled up to the curb right then. She spotted Jeannine, jumped out of the car, and dashed across the narrow grass strip separating the sidewalk from the curb. "Jeannine! You brought the baby. I'm so excited about that! And you!"

She grabbed hold of Jeannine and hugged her, then stepped back.

"We were just discussing the wedding this fall," said Jeannine, and Shirley twirled. It wasn't a girly twirl. Shirley played four years of basketball for the high school team, so her twirl was more of an athletic pivot on one foot.

Shirley raised her right hand. "I am a bridesmaid, and I will do the job justice," she drawled. "I shall embrace proper decorum for the entire day, without a lapse. So help me God."

"And the wedding shower." Cynthia directed a stern look at Shirley. "I want it dignified, Shirley."

"Like Malcolm!" Shirley raised her brows to widen her eyes, and it was hard to know if she was mocking or sincere.

Cynthia nailed her with a look. "Just like that. Brat."

"It will be beautiful," noted Jeannine. "I can't wait to see it. And if the shower is in September, I'll be sure to get time off so I can drive down on Friday. A whole weekend with my favorite people would be a wonderful thing."

She didn't mention her father or her stepmother.

She didn't have to.

She and Shirley had talked at length over the years, and Shirley understood that Hollis was still Hollis, but Jeannine kept herself outside their drama.

She was Susie's girl. That was how she saw herself, and in Regina's eyes, that was how she'd stay.

Chapter Twenty-Six

"It's just the three of us?" asked Shirley when she and Anne met Liam at the angel statue the next morning. "Evelyn is baking for the church's Easter bread exchange, and Joy can't get away from the gift shop because her volunteers are out sick. But where's Kevin?" she asked, glancing around. "He's late?"

A worry line creased Liam's brow. "I don't know. He sent me a cryptic text early this morning. Since then he hasn't responded to me."

Anne didn't like the sound of that. "Were you able to talk with him last night?"

"Yes." Liam winced. "Initially that was fine. He was going to meet us here this morning so we could compare notes. But I messed up," he confessed. "I told him we were looking into a possible connection between Chas Murrow and the lawyer that handled the adoption. The minute I said it, he got quiet."

"Bad quiet or thoughtful quiet?" asked Shirley.

"I'm guessing the former."

"Which means he went looking for them himself?" Anne searched the grounds extending out from the fountain, hoping Kevin would be walking their way. He wasn't. "Would he do that?"

"He was angry."

"Of course he was," said Anne, and she couldn't deny her worry. "He sacrificed everything to give those girls a safe life. To find out the cop he trusted and the lawyer who was supposed to be looking out for Emily's and Amelia's best interests were soaking families for money is infuriating. But where could he be?"

"That's just it. I don't know. He sent me this about two hours ago."

The text was time-stamped seven o'clock. TRACKING A LEAD. CAN'T MEET. PRAY I LEAVE THEM ALIVE.

Panic hit Anne. "Liam, we have to find him. I know he's angry, but he's going up against two men who have proven themselves to be heartless."

"And who duped him and ruined his daughters' chances to have a normal relationship with one another." Liam gripped the top of a nearby bench. "I don't know where to start. I have an address on Bausch but nothing on Murrow. He retired three years before I did. I used to tease him about his side jobs." Liam admitted this with a look of chagrin. "I didn't realize he really was pulling side jobs to pad his income."

"So we go to Bausch's house and rattle some chains," said Shirley.

Liam drove. They pulled up to Phil Bausch's beautiful home not far from Folly Beach. They walked up to the door, and Anne hit the bell with way more force than necessary.

A young man answered after a brief wait. He looked at the three of them and began closing the door. "We aren't all that religious around here, but thanks for stopping. Although there is a no solicitors sign on the post at the road."

"Where's your father?" Liam folded his arms and braced his legs, total cop. "I'm retired Detective Liam Holden, Atlanta PD, and I want to talk to Philip Bausch."

The young man frowned but didn't argue. "Detective, I respect law enforcement, but you just said you're out of your jurisdiction and retired."

Liam let that slide. "Where's your father right now? Trust me, when you mention that Liam Holden wants to talk to him about a certain adoption case, he'll come running."

The young man's eyes darkened. "My father did a lot of adoptions early in his career."

Shirley stepped in. "I can tell you're an educated young man. I saw your picture in the paper a few months ago when you were mentioned as one of Charleston's up-and-coming legal minds. But right now there's something much more serious and possibly sinister happening, and if you love your daddy at all, you'll find him for us."

The young man shook his head. "He's not here."

Liam scowled.

"He's not," he insisted. He was in his midtwenties, and there was an air of sincerity about him. "He took off in the Land Rover about two hours ago. He peeled out of the driveway, and if you knew my father and his love for cars, you'd know he never peels out. But he did. Is he in trouble? Really?" Genuine concern deepened the young man's voice. "I'm Ryan. His younger son. How can I help?" he went on. "I don't want anything to happen to my father."

"We don't want anything happening to anyone," Liam replied. "Call him. But don't say we're here."

Ryan pulled a phone from his pocket and hit a single key. A moment later, he connected with his father. "Dad. Hey, it's me. Where are you?"

Liam mouthed one word to him. "Speaker."

Ryan complied and hit the speaker button.

"I'll be back later, Ryan, but tell your mother to get things packed up for that vacation she's been wanting to take. It's an Easter surprise."

Anne stayed quiet, but it wasn't easy. Shirley's eyes went wide, then narrowed in indignation. Liam put a finger to his mouth and listened.

"We're going away?"

"Not you and George. I'm going to take Mom away for a bit once I get this job done."

"But where are you, Dad? You made a lot of noise taking off this morning."

"Had errands to run. Something I had to take care of. Gotta go. See you this afternoon."

He hung up.

Ryan faced Liam. "Something's wrong."

"I told you. How can we find him? Does that Land Rover have a GPS?"

Relief flooded Ryan's face. "It does. Do you have a Land Rover app?"

"Most retired cops don't drive Land Rovers," retorted Liam.

Ryan had the grace to look embarrassed. "Sorry. Download the app to your phone. I'll give you the code."

It took a moment, but when Liam's phone was hooked up with the information, he faced Ryan. "Don't warn him. Please. It's honestly a matter of life or death."

"He's my father."

"We know." Anne looked up into his worried face. "And he's made some bad mistakes, Ryan, but nothing worth dying over. Let us get to him. Talk to him. All right?"

They didn't have time to wait for an answer. They hurried back to the car. Liam drove. Anne rode shotgun and gave directions. The GPS indicated that the Rover was an hour away, and when Anne pulled up a map on her phone, her heart dropped.

She faced Liam. "We're going to the middle of a wildlife management area. Over in Colleton County."

"In other words, no people," noted Shirley.

"You ever been there?" asked Liam, and Anne shook her head.

"No. Shame on me, I don't tend to explore the local natural treasures like I should. There's all kinds of birds and critters and— No," she finished softly. "I'll be as lost as the two of you are."

"There must be roads."

"There are. Folks can stay on the roads and see things from their cars." She read the description of the wildlife management area, then paused. "This dot puts us in the middle of nowhere."

"Everywhere is somewhere." The absoluteness of Shirley's words should have made Anne feel better, but when she handed her phone back to her friend, Shirley's eyes went wide. And she swallowed hard. "Well, that is kind of nowhere, isn't it?"

"Can the car access it, I wonder?" asked Liam as they headed toward the county line.

Anne wasn't sure. "I don't know, Liam. It might be a gravel path leading to where this GPS is taking us. It's hard to discern it on the phone." The miniaturized size of the satellite map made her wish she'd upgraded to a bigger phone, but her small, old device fit into pockets. She hadn't anticipated tracking criminals when she'd bought it three years before.

"How far now?" Liam sounded worried.

"Far enough for a few prayers," said Shirley stoutly. "First, we're not even sure Kevin is with this Bausch man, and if he is, I can't imagine a smart lawyer wants murder added to his list of criminal activities."

"Except if no one knows where Kevin is or where he's been, how would they even look to find the body?"

"We'll tell them," Shirley said. "If we live through this, that is." She didn't seem worried, and the teasing note in her voice underscored that. "Besides, I'm happily anticipating Easter ham, so we'll just deal with whatever comes our way like we always do and look forward to celebrating the Good Lord's rising tomorrow."

"I like your confidence," Liam told her. He flashed a look in the rearview mirror back to Shirley. "But what if we're walking into something really bad here? I didn't think this through." He put his turn signal on to curve into a gas station just ahead before they ventured into thickly forested parkland. "I'm going to drop you ladies off here. Then I'll—"

"Oh no you won't," insisted Shirley in the no-nonsense voice she used for patients who didn't want to take their meds. It worked with them. Anne wasn't sure she wanted it to work now, because dropping them off didn't sound half bad as the darkness and depth of the forest lands loomed above the rural highway. "I don't hold with selling babies or splitting up families. I'm seeing this through."

Anne took a deep breath. It helped. "Me too. You're armed and we're smart." She reached over and patted Liam's shoulder. "We change the ratio, and that puts the odds in our favor. Drive on, Liam."

"Ladies, I—"

Anne consulted her map and pointed to the upcoming right turn. "Go right. Then once you get a fair distance up this road, find a way to go left, just beyond the wildlife management area. Somehow the Land Rover got back there. We've got to figure out a way to get there too. Kevin's done a lot of righteous deeds in his life. Let's do one in return."

Chapter Twenty-Seven

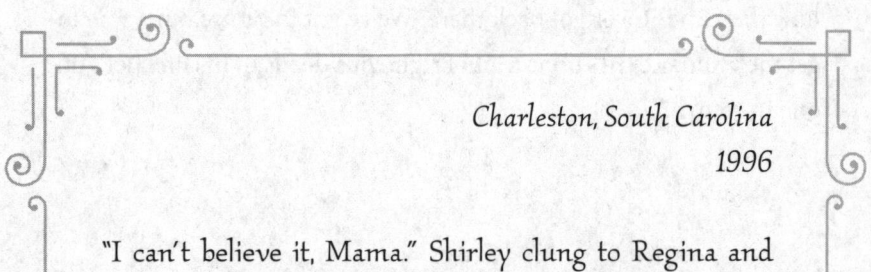

Charleston, South Carolina
1996

"I can't believe it, Mama." Shirley clung to Regina and didn't even try to hold back her tears. "I just can't believe it. Jeannine was my friend. She loved me even though she wasn't close by. She cared about me, and I cared about her, and I can't believe that folks can die having a baby when it's almost the twenty-first century. It makes no sense, Mama. None. And I am so mad at God right now. Very mad!"

Regina held tight.

Truth be told, she wasn't all that pleased with God at the moment either, because why would this happen? What was the point? That new baby barely a week old, left without a mother because Jeannine's heart gave out just a few days postdelivery.

Those two little girls, Emily and Amelia, with no mama, no grandma, and Kevin's family scattered around.

Regina was heartsore.

She'd promised Susie to look out for her girl. She'd made a firm commitment to a beloved friend that she'd be there for Jeannine, and she wasn't. She'd died alone in a hospital room with not one soul around, because everything had gone fine. Just fine. Until it didn't.

"I know, baby. I know. You cry, you rant, you do whatever you need to do. Just know your mama is feeling exactly the same way. She was a light in our lives for certain." She gripped Shirley around the shoulders and held her close, letting her cry and crying right along with her. "I know that light isn't truly gone. I know she's with her mama in heaven, but I also know there are two little girls who needed their mama right here on earth, so I don't pretend to understand why things happen the way they do."

She cried with her precious daughter.

They shared tissues. And later, when they were fixing supper, they shared a few stories, and then they cried again.

Regina made arrangements for her family to attend the funeral. They had to pay dearly for a hotel, because it was parents' weekend at local universities in and around Atlanta, and football season. The combination made weekend hotel rates skyrocket, but they'd pay the price for a night. She wasn't going to a precious woman's funeral in travel-weary clothes. No, sir. That wasn't how things were done.

Jeannine deserved that the folks who loved her would be there, best they were able, and pray. Not for pretty, talented, smart Jeannine. She was in God's arms. But for Kevin and those dear babies, because their arms were empty, and that should never, ever be the case.

Chapter Twenty-Eight

"Do you think Ryan warned his father?" asked Shirley.

Anne hoped not but she knew better. "My guess would be yes."

"Oh man. That gas station is suddenly looking better and better." Shirley fanned herself then stretched forward. "I have an idea," she said.

"Hold that thought," said Liam briskly. He paused the car, hit 911 on his phone, identified himself, and apprised a local operator of possible trouble in the woods to their left. When he hung up, he met Shirley's gaze. "At this point, backup is more important than worrying about a mob that might have nothing to do with any of this." He thrust the car back into gear. "I'm listening, Shirley." He moved ahead slowly while he and Anne scoured for a break in the trees.

"You're packing, right?" she asked Liam.

"You mean carrying a weapon? A gun? Yes."

"Let's drop you off. Anne and I will go in. Who's going to suspect two middle-aged women—"

"Gracious of you to include me in that category," noted Anne. She hadn't been middle-aged for a while.

"Folks are living longer all the time." Shirley exchanged a grin with Anne. "We drive in, we're lost. You sneak in with the gun if we need you."

"You think these men won't hesitate to take you down with Kevin?"

"I think there are so many folks that would be looking for us that it's unlikely, actually. They want a hidden crime," said Shirley sensibly. "Not a full-blown search. Two well-connected women disappearing into the wilderness of the preserve would cause a big stir, whereas a man under an assumed identity, thousands of miles from his home, wouldn't ruffle too many feathers. Folks would just assume he didn't know his way around the water."

Anne knew Shirley had won the argument when Liam slowed the car. "There is sense in what you say. And danger."

"Possibly," Anne said, "but if we seem lost and harmless, they might think we are. And we're just buying time, right? Until law enforcement arrives. They won't know about you."

"Unless the kid warned them."

"You're right," said Anne. "But if we all drive in there together, and your detective friend has a gun, we're all captured. Lili always told me when I worried about her in dangerous places that they knew how to divide and conquer and how everyone had each other's backs."

"I could use one of those regiments about now," said Shirley, but when Liam paused the car, she climbed out, fought the underbrush, and came around front. "Want to drive?" she asked Anne.

Anne shook her head. "I'll guide."

Liam slipped into the wooded area, and Shirley climbed into the driver's seat. He was taller, so she had to move the seat up. "Give me five minutes' head start," he instructed them.

"Will do. And you watch for us, you hear?" Anne replied. "Don't try to be a hero."

They gave Liam time to get closer to the teardrop-shaped red spot on Anne's map. Then Shirley eased forward on the narrow path. It wasn't graveled, and it would be a mud pit in the rain, but today it was plenty dry enough for the tires to grip and narrow enough that thin branches slapped the sides of Liam's car. Forest shadows blocked all except a little light, but as Shirley crept forward, the landscape brightened ahead.

"We're getting closer," whispered Anne.

"I see that. Now if you would be so good as to ignore what I'm about to say about your navigational skills and get that app off your phone." Shirley muttered the advice as the car came through the last curve of forest trail and into the light. Anne closed the app and popped open her door.

Shirley was amazing.

She ignored the possibly dangerous man racing their way, hopped out of the driver's seat, and put on one of the best shows Anne had ever seen. "I told you," she spouted as she stomped around the car, crossed her arms, and stamped her foot.

"I said no, this cannot be part of the wildlife tour, because no respectable wildlife would be hanging around a narrow path barely big enough for a whitetail deer much less a vehicle, but you insisted it would lead us right into the heart of bird country."

"It was the only road I saw," protested Anne. She blinked fast to show she was close to tears. "I don't know how we missed a turn, but we can just go back—"

"Through that narrow strip of dirt that's scratching up my car? That's your brilliant idea?" scolded Shirley. She turned as the man drew close. He eyed Anne and Shirley with a look of disbelief.

"It's my fault," Anne told him, and she pushed her lower lip out slightly. "I thought I was reading the map right, but I didn't see any other way into the management area, so I made her turn here."

"Please." Shirley put up one hand, palm out, as if to make Anne stop talking, so Anne did exactly that. Then Shirley faced the man as if it was perfectly normal to find him in the middle of nowhere. A deteriorating cabin stood at the back of the clearing. It was set on a slight knoll, high enough to avoid flooding. Beyond that, murky water soaked the roots of cattails and reeds, a perfect place to weight down a body for submersion. While there were people a scant twelve minutes away by car, they weren't likely to find their way up the weed-choked channel or through the thicket for any reason.

"Please tell me there's another way out," implored Shirley. "I can't believe I let her talk me into this on the day before Easter. And my car!" Shirley pointed at the scratches now marring the surface of Liam's black vehicle. "I can't believe this is happening. Please tell me there's another way back to the road."

"Who are you?" The man scowled at them.

Shirley ignored his expression altogether. "I'm Shirley. This is my friend Anne, or at least she used to be my friend before she brought me to the middle of nowhere." Shirley ended the short tirade with a sigh when Anne hiccupped a slight sob. "Now don't get riled, girl. I know stuff can get messed up even with GPS. Some of those signals go crazy in the woods and hills. I'm sorry." She dropped an overdone sigh into the conversation for effect. "It's not the end of the world."

"You're bird-watchers?" asked the man. Philip Bausch, assumed Anne, because Ryan bore a resemblance to him.

"We would be if we got to the right place," Shirley told him. "It's our first time."

"Shirley, can't we just turn the car around and head out the way we came in?" asked Anne. "I'll pay to have the car buffed out. It's my fault we're in this pickle."

"Well, I *was* driving," said Shirley, shouldering some of the blame.

Anne was running out of things to say.

Where was Liam? And where was Murrow? Was he here? Maybe their instincts were wrong. Or maybe—

And she hated to think it...

Kevin had already been killed.

Her heart did a weird beat in her chest, off-rhythm. She put her hand to her chest and Bausch noticed. "Are you about to have a heart attack on me?"

"Nerves, I expect. Just nerves." But then her heart did that weird little *thumpity-thump-thump* again, and she didn't try to hide her concern. "Or not. Is there a bathroom here? An outhouse, even? I'm not feeling so good."

"There's nothing here for you."

It was a different voice, coming from behind Anne. Another adrenaline rush hit her, and she hoped her slightly aged heart could withstand the overload of drama. She turned.

A second man was prodding Liam their way. He had Liam at gunpoint, and Liam's hands were bound behind him. For a moment Anne wondered if she could get to Liam's gun, but then she realized that Murrow—the man had to be Murrow—would have already taken it.

"Good night nurse, I think we've driven ourselves smack-dab into the middle of something we shouldn't have, Shirley!"

"So it would seem." Shirley kept her voice dry. "But—"

"Shut up." Murrow tossed a roll of duct tape to Bausch. "Take their phones and tie up their hands."

"Chas."

"Do it. We don't have time to mess around."

Murrow meant business.

Bausch looked unnerved. "This isn't part of the deal, Chas. You're talking four people here. Not one. And I'm not even good with one. You know that."

"You were good with a few million when all was said and done, though, weren't you?"

Bausch looked tormented, but he stood his ground. "Stealing isn't murder, Chas."

"What I know is that I didn't spend all my life working for what I have now to have it all disappear because a has-been detective and two old ladies—" He sent a disgusted look in Anne and Shirley's direction.

"I am not one bit old," said Shirley in a stout voice. "You take that back."

"I am," admitted Anne. "But it's still not a nice thing to say."

"Wait. Don't tie them." Murrow waved the gun toward the decrepit cabin. "Better that they find them without ligature marks of any kind. We've got the shutters closed, and the door locks up nice and tight. No way they're getting out before it burns down."

Burns?

Shirley shot a wide-eyed look at Anne.

Anne swallowed hard. Then she yelled. She yelled as loud and long as she could.

So did Shirley.

Murrow threw a hand across Shirley's mouth from behind.

Bausch did the same to Anne. With Murrow pointing the way with his gun, they made a solemn march to the cabin. It was then that Anne noticed a gas can. Big enough to hold two or three gallons of gasoline. Enough to torch a dried-out cabin in the middle of nowhere.

The cabin had a couple of visible windows and a front door. The front door didn't have a traditional key. It had a piece of wood that could be slid up and down into a wooden notch like an old-time prairie cabin.

Bausch pushed the wood up—Anne wasn't well-versed on wood, but this looked like a classic piece of 2×4. Not easily moved or maneuvered. When the door popped open, there was Kevin Eddington, hunched in the corner. His feet and wrists were bound, and a wide swatch of the silvery tape covered his mouth.

"Looks like you've got company," snarled Murrow as he pushed Liam into the room. "If you were hoping not to die alone, your wish just came true. By the time anybody finds you, we'll be out of the country, although I would have been happier to stay here, living life. But then Big Daddy over there had to come looking and stir things up. That was a mistake on your part," Murrow told Kevin. "A big one. We didn't come this far to be brought down because you suddenly had a qualm of conscience about giving your kids away twenty-five years ago."

"Feel free to untie him," Murrow ordered Shirley as he backed out the door. "Both of them. And give me the tape. I don't want it lying around. No sense leaving evidence. We'll just let folks think you were all stupid enough to lock yourselves in. Phil, go get the stuff and put it in the Land Rover. Make sure there's nothing left that can lead back to us."

"Chas." The lawyer swept the four people a look of indecision. "We can't do this. Instead, just leave them here. By the time they get found, we'll be gone. You said yourself, they can't get out. Smoke from a fire could bring folks around quicker."

For a moment Murrow looked as if he was going to agree. But then his phone beeped with a text message. He glanced at his phone, grimaced, and took a last step out the door. "Burn it."

The door pulled shut with the snap of wood against wood. Then the sound of the 2×4 being pushed into place came through.

Kevin crossed to one window. Liam tried the other. The glass was half-gone, but the solid wood shutters outside seemed impenetrable, and the back door was nailed shut.

There really was no way out.

Anne stared around the musty cabin.

It was older than it had appeared outside. Much older. An old-style pump-handle sink stood near one corner. A couple of rickety shelves were hung above it, and a few old nails protruded from the slab wood walls.

She stared at the makings of what must have been a miniature kitchen, then looked at the floor. While Kevin, Liam, and Shirley tried various ways to get the shutters open, Anne ran her fingers along the dark and dusty slabs of wood. She was about to give up when her fingers touched something. Something small and round. And near the rounded peg-like knob was a thin groove that ran left and right.

She pulled on the rounded edge.

Nothing happened.

Anne pulled harder.

Still nothing. "Kevin. Liam. Come here, quick!"

The men crossed to her and bent low.

"Pull this knob," she told them. "I think there's a root cellar under this, but the doorway is stuck. Pull hard."

They did. First Liam. Then Kevin. And then Liam got an idea. He smashed an old wooden chair against a wall. The dry wood broke apart. He picked up one of the splintered pieces and pushed the thin edge down along the side of the wood nearest the knob and then—

With him prying and Kevin pulling...

The door finally opened.

It was pitch black below. There was no way of knowing if they were descending to their death or waiting for it at ground level, so they went down the rickety ladder.

Anne felt around. Shelves lined one side. She slid her hand across the shelf, praying there were no snakes, until her hand hit several rounded tapered items. "Candles," she whispered.

Kevin had pulled the access door back down via a small hank of rope on the underside of the plank. There was no way for Murrow or Bausch to see inside the building without opening a door or a shutter, and there was no reason for them to do that. Anne hoped that bought them time. Liam was passing his hand back and forth along the deeper set shelves. He groaned softly.

"Are you all right?" Shirley whispered.

"Mouse. Long dead. I'm fine."

Liam took a small flashlight out of his pocket and shot the beam around the space. When he took it to the farthest end of the root cellar, he whistled lightly. "A door."

"Really?" Anne tried to peer through the shadows, but the darkness and Kevin blocked her view.

"Leading to something even more exciting?" asked Shirley, ever practical.

Kevin snapped his fingers. "Leading outside, I bet."

"No." Shirley looked dubious.

"Sure," he replied. "The cabin is on a hill. And the backside faces the water. I expect there's a root cellar entrance on the creek side. Chilled water kept things fresh, right? I'm pretty sure I heard that in seventh-grade American history."

Liam reached out to turn the handle.

It didn't budge.

He tried harder.

Still nothing.

"Let's both try," suggested Kevin. "On three." He counted to three, and just as they were about to bruise their shoulders, Anne spotted a key hanging high on the doorframe.

"Guys. Hey."

They paused and looked back. She lifted her phone's light toward the key above Liam's head. "Let's try that instead."

Liam rolled his eyes, lifted the key off a nail, and handed it to Kevin.

It fit. It took a couple of tries to line the door and the frame up for the key to work, but within thirty seconds they had pushed open the door just enough to get out. Kudzu vines formed a thick drape across the narrow pass on the other side of the door. The green vines obscured the view, but Anne could peer through the leaves to see activity on the other side of the clearing.

Phil was packing something into the Land Rover. She couldn't tell what. Behind them, and above, gasoline-fired smoke began pouring into the air. They were far enough out of the cellar to be safe, but close enough to realize how dangerous these men truly were.

And then, without a backward glance at the burning building and the four people inside, Chas Murrow climbed into the Land Rover.

Philip Bausch didn't.

Murrow yelled something. The roar of the burning timbers obscured the words, but Anne saw Bausch turn and run back toward the building.

"He wants to free us," whispered Shirley.

But then Murrow pulled a gun once more. He aimed it at Bausch's back. "Get in the car now or you're done, Phil. It's all done. There are no do-overs when you're in this deep."

Liam started forward, but just as he was about to push through the vines to try to save Bausch's life, a voice and a shot rang out of the woods. "Colleton County Sheriff. Put the gun down and your hands in the air. I repeat, put the gun down and your hands up."

Bausch kept going toward the burning building. "We've got to save them," he yelled back over his shoulder. "Now!"

Weapons drawn, half a dozen sheriff's deputies poured out of the woods. Relief surged through Anne. "We're here!" she yelled from beneath the blanket of bright green kudzu. "We're safe!"

Two sheriffs had gotten Murrow out of the driver's seat and were pulling his hands into handcuffs behind his back.

Bausch was still running, terror on his face. When he saw Anne and the others, his relief was palpable. He dropped to his knees, and Anne saw the difference between the two criminal minds.

Murrow would have let them die a horrible death, but Bausch risked his life so that wouldn't happen.

As the deputies put Philip Bausch in handcuffs, she wondered if Murrow would have killed him.

The thought that he probably would have was sobering.

But then Kevin put an arm around her shoulders from the other side, and an even greater truth rang free.

They'd saved this man's life. She wasn't sure how, but they had, and that made the risk worth the reward. When a man was willing to sacrifice so much to keep his children safe, that showed great depth of character. The kind of character the staff noted in Katie and Kitty Sue. They worked hard, did what was right, and gave it their best.

He'd done that. And now his daughters would have a chance to say thank you.

Chapter Twenty-Nine

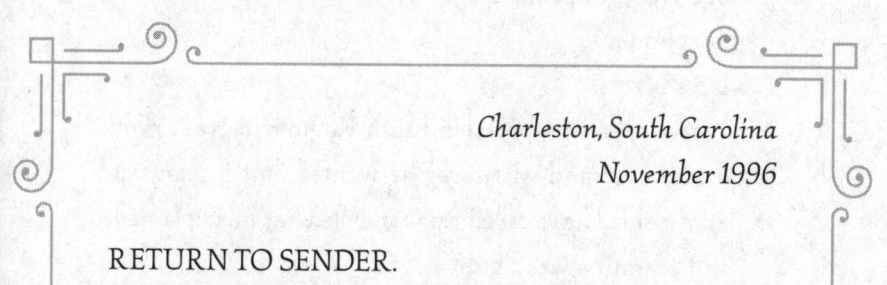

Charleston, South Carolina
November 1996

RETURN TO SENDER.

The postal message was splayed across Kevin and Jeannine's address. Not as if Kevin hadn't wanted the encouraging card, but as if he no longer lived on Wildwood Road in Cumming, Georgia.

Regina flipped the returned envelope over and frowned.

Kevin wasn't a phone person. Jeannine used to say he spent too much time on the phone at work, and Regina understood that. Charles was the same way about weekend appointments, because his life was governed by appointments five days a week. Thirty-minute increments of this, that, and the other thing, so he liked his Sundays and Mondays to be free whenever possible.

She'd sent cards and notes each week since Jeannine's passing, but this one—a heartfelt prayerful card with an eye toward the difficulty of holidays without Jeannine—never got opened.

She called his number.

It wasn't Kevin that answered, or even invited her to leave a message. That would be normal. No. Instead, a smooth but automated voice accepted the call with a standard turn-back message. "We're sorry, but that number has been disconnected."

No phone.

No address.

A spot of panic nipped her heart. Kevin had every right to go wherever and whenever he wanted, but if Jeannine were alive, she'd have called Regina. Filled her in. Explained.

But Jeannine wasn't alive.

She called directory assistance to get the number for Kevin's firm. Then she rolled her shoulders and dialed his office. She wasn't one to interrupt a man when he was working, but if this was the only way to check on him and the girls, so be it.

"I'm sorry." An easy-talking woman with no trace of a Southern drawl answered her request to talk to Kevin. "Mr. Eddington is no longer employed at Applewaite, Applewaite, Sterling & Kush."

No phone. No address. No job.

The panic in her chest moved to her gut.

She dialed his phone again, not knowing what could possibly change, but hoping for a different result.

Nope. Same stupid recording saying that number was no longer assigned.

She didn't know their neighbors on Wildwood Road, but Thelma Jackson's son was in the sheriff's department there. She called Thelma, got Brayson's number, and called him. "Brayson, can you just check out their house? I'm worried about what's going on," she confessed when he answered the phone. "A man that's grieving the way Kevin is might be normal most times, but grief changes things. It turns them around and shakes them upside down until a body might not know if they're coming or going, and he's got two little girls. A toddler and an infant. I'm heartsick I can't get ahold of him."

"I'll check it out, Miss Regina."

He called back an hour later. "The house is for sale."

The anxiety magnified. "He's moving?"

"Moved would be my guess," Brayson continued. "Locked up tight and nothing in the house that I can see. No furniture, nothing on the counters. Looks empty."

An empty house, up for sale. No phone. No job. No trace of Kevin anywhere. What if he wasn't all right? What if something happened to the girls? "Brayson, I'm worried sick."

"I hear that, Miss Regina. Let me check further and see if I dig anything up. Can't hurt to try."

She prayed.

Oh, how she prayed!

She prayed for Kevin's peace of mind, for the girls' safety, for their well-being. And when Brayson called her forty-eight hours later and told her he'd found no trace of Kevin or the girls anywhere, her heart broke.

She'd made a promise to her beloved friend. She'd promised to look out for Jeannine. To stay in touch, and she had, but then precious Jeannine died alone—*all alone*—and her beloved husband and daughters were nowhere to be found.

It was impossible.

And yet real. Too real. Gone, without a trace, without a nod, without a breath of goodbye.

Just gone, and Regina felt like she'd not only failed Susie, she'd failed Jeannine and her girls.

She'd just completed a double shift. A tiny baby boy had come to their upgraded and updated NICU late that night, a baby that wouldn't have been saved twenty years before but had a good shot at making it now. She'd not only watched change happen, she was part of the change. Part of the team. She'd spent last evening and the whole night crooning to babies, tending their needs, adjusting their tiny limbs.

She put her hands on life-giving therapies every day, but right now none of that seemed to matter, because all she could do was think of Susie, Jeannine, and those girls...

All gone but never forgotten.

With a heavy heart, she sat down and cried. Then prayed. Then cried while she was praying, and by the time she finally fell asleep to be ready for her next overnight shift, the sun had gone down.

Heartbroken, she fell asleep, but it wasn't the sweet and easy sleep she knew firsthand.

It was broken. Just like her heart. And Regina had no idea how to put it back together again.

Chapter Thirty

The sheriffs had taken Murrow and Bausch away. Anne and the others followed in Liam's car. They gathered at the county sheriff's office, where two FBI agents awaited them.

When they were all done with interviews, Shirley came out of one office while Liam exited another. They came toward Anne and Kevin.

Then Shirley drew up short. She looked at Kevin. Really looked. And then she looked again.

He lifted both brows in question. "Something wrong?"

She started to shake her head as if confused, then reached out and grabbed hold of his hands. "You're Jeannine's husband."

It was his turn to look surprised. "How do you know that?"

"I'm Regina's daughter. Her younger one. Shirley. My mama loved your wife. And Susie, her mother."

Kevin stared at her in disbelief. "You can't be."

"I am," she insisted, and Anne and Liam watched as she clung tight to Kevin's hands. "The last time I saw Jeannine was when she was expecting Amelia."

"Shirley, I had no idea." He looked befuddled and happy and rather dumbfounded.

"Now you do," Shirley declared. "And Kevin Eddington, you've got to come home to supper with us. My mama will be beside herself to see you, and oh my land"—the surprise on Shirley's face deepened—"when she realizes that those girls have been here all along, working alongside me, she will be over the moon. She made a promise to Jeannine's mother that she would watch over Jeannine. When Jeannine died so suddenly, my mama got it in her head that she'd let her old friend down. Why, just last week Mama came to Mercy to visit the shot clinic and she spotted Katie having lunch. The moment she laid eyes on her, she said how Katie reminded her of her old friend's daughter. I shrugged it off. Shame on me! Oh goodness, Kevin, this story will make my mama cry and cheer."

"Your mother never let anyone down," said Kevin, but disbelief still colored his expression. "Jeannine had so many stories, and the best and most beautiful ones revolved around Regina Bashore. But I don't want to intrude. Maybe almost getting you all killed was enough, eh?"

"Intrude?" Shirley reached out and wrapped him in a big hug. "You're like family to us. A prodigal, coming home. My mama has never stopped praying for you and those girls, and her prayers were answered in the best way. One way or another they brought you back here to meet your daughters. Can we do it tonight?" she asked. "I know it's Easter tomorrow—"

"I don't know how Kitty Sue's family would feel about it, but Sunny and Drake would be fine with it," said Liam. "I called them. They're glad we're alive to tell the story but also thrilled that we got to the bottom of it. Katie won't have to worry about anything anymore."

"Maybe we shouldn't spring this on Kitty Sue's parents," cautioned Anne. "They don't—"

Clearly Katie didn't agree with Anne's more cautious reasoning, because a text chime came through Anne's and Shirley's phones simultaneously. They both looked down. And then Anne breathed a sigh of relief as she held up the picture for all to see. SISTERS! it said, and the selfie of Katie and Kitty Sue, Kevin and Jeannine's precious Emily and Amelia, showed their brilliant smiles and their resemblance to the woman who gave her life giving them theirs. JUST COULDN'T WAIT TO TELL HER! texted Katie. CAN'T STOP LAUGHING. AND HUGGING!

Tears filled Kevin's eyes. Then they spilled over as he looked at his daughters—his girls—together as sisters for the first time in over twenty-five years. And when Anne handed him a tissue, he wiped his eyes and nodded. "Yes. I'll come. Now that I've been told by the authorities that the mob had nothing to do with this and my daughters are safe, I want to meet them. And their parents. And I want to say thank you to them for giving my girls the safety and security and normalcy I couldn't."

Anne's eyes filled. Shirley dabbed at hers too. Even Liam was red-eyed. He slapped Kevin's shoulder. "Ride with me," he said. "We'll give the ladies time to set things up, okay? And let's get coffee. I might have been tempted to something stronger, but not on Holy Saturday. Sunrise service in the morning."

"I'll text you," Shirley promised. "And I'll get home to Mama and fill her in. She'll be so excited, Kevin. She doesn't always remember what she had for breakfast, but she's never forgotten all that happened back then." She hugged him again, and when she let him go, she took a firm step back and clung to his hand. "Welcome home, Kevin. Welcome home."

Liam drove them back to Anne's car. They decided to gather at Anne's house because it was bigger, and with several families meeting, they needed space.

Ralph ordered food.

Evelyn said she'd bring several loaves of Easter bread.

Joy had made an extra cake for the holiday, just in case. She brought it along and helped set things up as Kevin pulled up to the curb a few houses down the road. Anne was about to go meet him when Ralph put a hand on her shoulder. "When we're done with this happy reunion, we're going to talk about my wife risking her life."

A mix of love and concern darkened his gentle gaze. She faced him and put her hands on his shoulders. "This from a man who quotes the book of Daniel and preaches about sacrificial love to help folks be better versions of themselves? That den of lions meant business, my love, and God delivered Daniel, didn't He?"

He grimaced because he'd offered many a sermon pairing Daniel's faith in the den of lions with New Testament scripture. She reached up and gave him a big hug. "I didn't mean to worry you, and you're right—we didn't expect that level of danger. But we didn't walk in cold, Ralph. We had police backup. In the end, Kevin escaped with his life to be reunited with his long-lost daughters because we took a measured risk. I believed that the sheriff's department would have our backs. And they did."

"I want you safe, Anne."

"I know." She smiled up at him. "Me too. We've got a lot of life to live, Ralph, and I aim to live it together. And now—"

She turned back toward Kevin. He was making his way up the street. He looked nervous. She was about to walk his way when Ralph spoke again. "Let me. Give us a little father-to-father time."

"Good idea." She patted his hand and watched her wonderful husband go to meet a man whose life had taken so many unalterable turns. Ralph didn't go down the sidewalk. He crossed the lawn to meet Kevin faster, and when the two men stood there talking the way men do, she knew Ralph was the right man for the job. They came her way as Evelyn and James arrived together in James's car.

Evelyn moved forward first and clasped Kevin's hand. "A part of me was sorry to have missed this morning's adventure right up until I found out what happened. For once I'm all right with hearing about the ending in retrospect!"

Kevin laughed as he shook James's hand. "It was scary. I don't think I've ever been so angry in my life, that anyone could sell children to benefit their bank accounts when their mother and I would have done anything to keep the girls safe."

"And you did."

"And now they know they're sisters, so they can actually be sisters," added Joy in a bright tone. "And not just look like it."

Two cars came their way. Liam drove the first car. A woman sat beside him, and behind them was a middle-aged couple. Anne assumed they were Sunny and Drake. But no Katie.

Anne took a breath.

The other car pulled in behind the Holdens.

The couple in the front seat was a little younger than Sunny and Drake. And then, as Liam and his family exited their car, the back doors of the other car flew open and two excited young women—who looked an awful lot like their late mother—piled out of the car like kids at a playground.

They didn't wait. They didn't hesitate. They didn't pause. They raced across the lawn and threw their arms around Kevin. They hugged him so hard they almost bowled him over. And for long, tear-filled moments, they didn't let go. When they did, Katie gazed up at him and simply said, "Hey, Dad. I'm Emily. Aka Katie."

"Which makes me Amelia," quipped Kitty Sue.

The look on Kevin's face was priceless.

Tears ran down his cheeks. And down theirs. And when they finally stopped hugging, it was as if the girls couldn't move away from him. As if now that they understood the reasons behind their adoptions and the shenanigans that instigated their separation, they didn't want to be parted again.

Kevin didn't just shake the parents' hands. He hugged them. Thanked them. And then hugged them again.

It was a beautiful evening. Quiet. Warm but not hot. Pleasant and comforting. They settled in the backyard for appetizers and conversation. There was no shortage of either.

The girls kept looking at their dad.

He kept looking at them as if he couldn't quite believe his eyes.

Then he turned.

Stopped.

Stared.

His throat convulsed as Regina came around the corner of the house.

He didn't make her cross the distance alone.

He hurried across the wide yard to hug her.

More tears.

More tissues.

More emotion.

And when Regina finally drew back, she reached up and bracketed Kevin's face with her hands. "I have missed you and those girls for so long, Kevin Eddington, but when my Shirley told me what you did to save their lives and to put dangerous folks in jail, I had not one bit of trouble believing it because"—she swept the gathered people a knowing and warm look—"I knew the kind of man you were even way back then, the very best kind for our dear Jeannine. And you are still that same man. Welcome home, Kevin." She repeated the words Shirley had uttered a few short hours ago and hugged Kevin again. "Welcome home."

Dear Reader,

I loved writing this story. I enjoy writing mysteries, but this one in particular grabbed me because I got to combine two favorites: babies and biological science. I have always been fascinated by biology, how the body forms, what can go wrong and how often it goes right. (Somehow not one of my six children inherited my love for biology, science, medicine, etc. Not one. I'm not sure how that happened!) Pairing that love for biology and babies is a natural lead-in for Special Care Nurseries (now NICUs) and the amazing intercessions that keep babies growing even when they emerge from the womb too soon.

    Now, with DNA testing, we can see lineage more clearly. This is good and bad in a private adoption because sometimes the reasons for privacy go beyond human choice and straight to danger. And that was the case in this book. When folks go into witness protection, they're not offered a window of time for goodbyes. Seeing one another again isn't likely to happen unless the threat is eradicated. Weaving the past through the present and keeping Shirley away from Kevin until the end was all part of making sure the mystery worked within the confines of the circumstances. And it worked…sensibly! And that made me happy! Thank you so much for reading *Merciful Secrecy*. In this case, Emily and Amelia were the reasons for secrecy, and it was God's timing that brought the secret and the girls back into the open. And Kevin's joy at seeing his girls again... Well, that made everything else worthwhile!

I love chatting with readers! Email me at loganherne@gmail.com, visit ruthloganherne.com, or friend me on Facebook. Sending you hugs and blessings from our family's pumpkin farm!

Signed,
Ruthy

About the Author

MULTIPUBLISHED, BESTSELLING, AND AWARD-WINNING author Ruth Logan Herne is living her dream of writing and publishing novels, running a farm, telling fourteen grandkids "No!" and "Stop that!" (a favorite line from *Steel Magnolias*), baking for her farm market, fixing things that break, and watching brilliant athletes perform on local Little League and soccer fields. An avid baker, Ruthy has worn many hats, hairnets, and name tags in her multitude of jobs over the years, but she's pretty sure that just makes her stories more real!

The Story Behind the Story

From Sideshow to NICU

THE PAST TRODS THE HEELS of the present, doesn't it?

Regina Bashore's life as a Special Care Nursery nurse reads like a time machine for the NICU. A century ago, there was little to be done for babies born too soon. Few doctors took action, and tightly budgeted hospitals wanted proof that interventions worked. Parents were left afloat on a sea of uncertainty, governed by lack of knowledge.

Dr. Martin Couney provided the seeds of hope by offering access to his incubators free of charge so that parents of preemies could have their babies housed in a warmed environment. Sounds good, right?

But here's the catch: The incubators were a sideshow at Coney Island, New York! His sideshows inspired similar exhibits at European expositions, the New York World's Fair of 1933, and the Chicago World's Fair of 1939.

That oddity became the cornerstone for today's NICU. With proof that controlling temperature and humidity worked, further developments brought oxygen into the Isolettes. Staff realized that handwashing impeded staph infections, and the change from total isolation for babies to well-staffed units with babies housed together took hold. Eventually parents were welcome to come in, hold their special needs infants, rock them, sing to them. Today's norm may have begun in circus sideshow style, but it's become a cornerstone that's saved millions of tiny lives.

Regina's story reflects that history of change. Her work in Mercy Hospital made her a pioneer. She watched and worked firsthand as technology was developed to save tiny lives that would have been lost a few decades back. The work of hands like Regina's has made a difference to those precious babies that come too soon and to their worried parents, and not in a traveling sideshow. Babies are now nurtured and cared for by the best possible means in NICUs across our nation. And that's a wonderful step up from midway baby care.

Good for What Ails You

Dessert Croissants

This fancy pastry using store-bought croissants is easy to make and sure to impress any time of year. Make the custard ahead of time and chill it thoroughly. Croissants can be stuffed up to a day ahead of time and refrigerated until serving. You need croissants, strawberries, homemade custard, and whipped cream.... A fancy dessert in quickstep time!

Buy 1 dozen small croissants. (Time saved!)
  Split them in half lengthwise, leaving a top and bottom.
  Fill with custard.
  Cover custard with sliced strawberries.
  Dollop whipped cream onto berries. Put top in place. Dust with powdered sugar.

Custard:

2 tablespoons butter, melted	2 cups milk
¾ cup sugar	2 egg yolks
¼ cup cornstarch	1 teaspoon vanilla

Melt butter in 3-quart saucepan. Mix sugar and cornstarch together, then mix with melted butter in saucepan. Whisk in milk and egg yolks. Heat over medium heat, stirring fairly constantly until mixture thickens and comes to a boil. Remove from heat. Add vanilla. Chill thoroughly.

Whipped Cream:
- 1 pint heavy cream
- ⅓ cup sugar

Whip heavy cream and sugar in a big bowl until volume increases and the whipped cream will hold a firm peak. Chill.

Layer croissants as instructed, dust with powdered sugar, and refrigerate until serving.

Read on for a sneak peek of another exciting book in the Sweet Carolina Mysteries series!

Sunken Hopes
BY GABRIELLE MEYER

EVELYN PERRY STUDIED THE MUSEUM blueprints, trying to appear busy, but her attention wasn't on the piece of paper in her hands or even the carpenters working around her. All she could think about was the appointment she had scheduled in ten minutes.

The sound of hammers, power drills, and conversation filled the large room in the Angel Wing of Mercy Hospital. Skilled workers constructed display cases, complete with solid maple bases and plexiglass lids. Soon, those cases would be filled with the artifacts that Evelyn and her team of curators had painstakingly selected for the past couple of months. Items that would tell the complex and unique history of the famous Charleston hospital.

"Evelyn!" Anne Mabry entered the new museum, her eyes wide with curiosity and excitement. She was a dedicated volunteer at Mercy Hospital and a good friend of Evelyn's. She was just as enthusiastic about the museum as Evelyn. "This room looks amazing. I can't believe the transformation."

Evelyn smiled at her friend as she set aside the blueprints, eager to give Anne a personal tour. "What do you think of the color we selected for the walls and carpet? Too bland?"

Anne's gaze slid over the room. Evelyn had chosen a charcoal-colored carpet, made for heavy foot traffic, and paired it with creamy gray on the walls. Large plate glass windows looked out at the Grove, a beautiful green space along the side of the hospital. They were still in the midst of the installation phase, but Evelyn had been assured that the carpenters would be finished today. They were putting last-minute touches on the exhibit panels, display cases, and lighting. All the room needed now were the actual artifacts that would tell the story.

"I think it's perfect," Anne said, slipping her shoulder-length blond hair behind one ear. "I still can't believe this is becoming a reality. After all this time."

Evelyn inhaled a deep breath, reveling in the sights and smells of the remodeled space. She'd dreamed of adding a museum to the hospital for years, and finally, six months ago, they'd been given the green light from the hospital board after Evelyn received a substantial grant to see the project completed. It hadn't been easy, since she was still expected to work her regular job as the supervisor of the records department, but she'd made it happen.

The door to the museum opened again, and this time Joy Atkins and Shirley Bashore entered. Their expressions matched Anne's, making Evelyn feel proud of the work they had accomplished in such a short time.

Joy was the manager of the hospital gift shop, and Shirley was a float nurse who worked wherever her expertise was needed. Both of them were relatively new to Mercy but had quickly become friends with Evelyn and Anne.

"This looks wonderful," Joy said to Evelyn. "And to think, this used to be an old storage room at one time."

"A storage room, hospital rooms, an old entrance," Evelyn amended. "There's almost no way of knowing all the ways this space was used for the past two hundred years." The Angel Wing of Mercy Hospital had a fascinating history. Built in 1829, with beautiful red brick and charming gables, it had stood the test of time. It was nestled in the midst of the historic district in Charleston Harbor and served as the general hospital for the local citizens, though it was also a popular tourist destination because of its past. When a fire tore through Charleston during the Civil War, everyone thought the building was lost. But when the ashes settled and the rubble was cleared, the citizens discovered that the Angel Wing, with its beautiful Angel of Mercy statue, had been spared.

The structure had been rebuilt and modernized over the past two centuries, but the statue and the historic wing were preserved. Daily, tourists drove by, trying to get a peek at the statue. Rumors abounded about hidden tunnels, secret passageways, and unexplained miracles.

What better place to put the museum?

It didn't hurt that it was right across the hall from the records department, giving Evelyn easy access.

"We know you're busy," Shirley said to Evelyn, "but do you have time to give us a little tour during our lunch break?"

Evelyn glanced at her watch. "I have an important meeting in a few minutes, but I can show you around until Mr. Lorenzo arrives."

"We don't want to keep you," Joy said.

"The meeting will be here," Evelyn explained. "And you might like to attend, if you have the time."

"Sounds intriguing." Anne lifted her eyebrows as she glanced at each of her friends and then back to Evelyn. "Who's Mr. Lorenzo?"

Evelyn could barely contain her excitement, feeling like a child about to open a much-anticipated birthday or Christmas present. "The director of the Warren Lasch Conservation Center."

"Isn't that where they have the Civil War submarine?" Shirley asked, squinting her dark brown eyes. "I took Mama there this past summer. It was fascinating."

"You're right," Evelyn said. "The submarine is the *H.L. Hunley*. The conservation center has a special artifact they're loaning to us for the grand opening. We'll keep it through the summer, cross-promoting the two museums."

"That's exciting." Joy's face lit up with interest. "Is the governor still coming to the grand opening?"

Evelyn's pulse ticked a little higher at the reminder. "He is, which is all the more reason I'm anxious to get all the artifacts in place." She led her friends away from the door and into the heart of the exhibit floor. The natural lighting from the tall, tinted windows, combined with the museum track lighting, gave the room a warm, comfortable feel. A team of museum specialists from the South Carolina Historical Society had been working closely with Evelyn and were currently helping the carpenters with display cases.

The plan was to start installing the artifacts tomorrow, though it would take over two weeks to complete. Evelyn hoped to have a few days on the other side of the installation to do a final cleaning before the grand opening.

The exhibit panels, with information about the history of the hospital and how it had impacted Charleston, were already installed. They were impressive, made of top-quality materials.

"I couldn't have done any of this without the South Carolina Historical Society," Evelyn said to her friends. "They've been wonderful to work with and so professional."

"It's easy to see they know what they're doing." Shirley stopped to admire a panel that showed the history of the Angel of Mercy statue. A life-size picture of the statue was set against a beautiful blue sky. "This is such a great addition to the hospital. Well done, Evelyn."

Evelyn's cheeks warmed. "It's a team effort, to be sure."

"But it was born from your vision." Anne squeezed Evelyn's arm affectionately.

The main door opened, and Evelyn glanced up to see Cyril Lorenzo enter with a small metal case in his hand.

"He's here," Evelyn said, her voice betraying her excitement.

The others looked in the same direction but stayed back as Evelyn went to greet her special visitor.

"Hello, Mr. Lorenzo."

"It's nice to see you again, Mrs. Perry. I've brought the coin."

The lead curator from the South Carolina Historical Society, Adam Chilton, joined Evelyn and shook Mr. Lorenzo's hand. Adam was a thirtysomething with a shock of dark hair and black-rimmed glasses. He'd been excited to help Evelyn from the beginning and was instrumental in working out the loan from the conservation center when he learned the connection between the twenty-dollar gold coin they possessed and the reconstruction of Mercy Hospital after the fire.

"Where would you like it?" Mr. Lorenzo asked him.

"Over here." Adam indicated that everyone should follow him. He led them to a corner of the museum, sectioned off with plastic hanging from the ceiling. There, he was housing some of the other artifacts that had already been returned to the hospital. Over the years, Mercy had loaned out their antiques to neighboring museums and historic sites. With Adam's help, Evelyn had started to recall the loans. For the most part, the other organizations were happy to hear about the hospital museum and had gladly returned the items. But there were still some who were sore about the recalls.

Evelyn wasn't worried about those pieces today. Instead, she gave her full attention to Mr. Lorenzo and the gold coin he was about to reveal to them.

Adam cleared off one of the tables where he'd been documenting artifacts and indicated that Mr. Lorenzo could set the case down.

Evelyn stood nearby, while Anne, Joy, and Shirley stayed near the plastic wall, out of the way.

"You've taken all the proper precautions with security?" Mr. Lorenzo asked Adam and Evelyn, his gaze serious.

"We have," Evelyn assured him. "All the locks are in place, as well as security cameras on all the exits to this room. No one will touch the artifacts unless they are preapproved members of the team. Adam and I will personally oversee anyone who handles the coin."

Mr. Lorenzo nodded and then had Evelyn sign several forms before he was ready to open the case.

Everyone looked on eagerly as he unlatched the box and lifted the lid.

Nestled in a bed of black velvet was a Civil War–era twenty-dollar gold coin, indented from a bullet and inscribed on the back. It said: *April 6, 1862, My Life Preserver.*

"Why is the coin so special?" Joy asked in a hushed tone.

Mr. Lorenzo stepped aside so the women could get a better look and said, "It was given to Lieutenant George E. Dixon by his sweetheart, Queenie Bennett, before he left to fight in the war. She gave it to him in case he needed supplies, but he kept it in his pocket, as a way to remember her."

"That's sweet," Anne said.

Mr. Lorenzo continued. "Family legend says that during the Battle of Shiloh he was shot, but the bullet hit the coin, thereby sparing his life. In 1864, Dixon became the captain of the *H.L. Hunley,* the first successful submarine used in warfare, right here in the Charleston Harbor. Unfortunately, after the submarine fired a torpedo and took down a Union ship, it never resurfaced, and the story of the coin became a legend."

"That *is* unfortunate," Joy agreed. "I've heard of the submarine but haven't had a chance to learn more."

"For over a century," Evelyn said, "no one knew what happened to the submarine the night it went on its last mission. I think it was 1995 when they finally discovered it about a hundred yards away from where the Union ship was torpedoed, in only twenty-seven feet of water. Several feet of silt buried it and protected it from damage. About twenty years ago, they lifted it from the water and started preserving it at the conservation center. The archaeologists discovered the damaged coin with Lieutenant Dixon's remains, proving the family legend was true."

"And how does this coin connect to Mercy Hospital?" Shirley asked Evelyn.

"The Dixon family donated a great sum of money to help rebuild the hospital after the fire, in remembrance of Lieutenant Dixon. They were benefactors for many years, though we lost touch with them in the early twentieth century." She smiled with excitement. "I've been in contact with one of the Dixon family members, though, and she's coming tomorrow to see the exhibit."

They continued to admire the coin for several minutes, and then the women dispersed back to their jobs within the hospital, leaving Evelyn alone with Adam and Mr. Lorenzo.

Before Mr. Lorenzo left, he gave Evelyn a long glance. "I am entrusting this to your care, Mrs. Perry."

"Yes, I know." She smiled. "I will guard it with all precaution."

"See that you do." He nodded once and then left the museum.

Despite Evelyn's assurance, she suddenly felt the weight of her responsibility.

The coin was irreplaceable. What if something happened to it?

A Note from the Editors

WE HOPE YOU ENJOYED ANOTHER exciting volume in the Sweet Carolina Mysteries series, published by Guideposts. For over seventy-five years, Guideposts, a nonprofit organization, has been driven by a vision of a world filled with hope. We aspire to be the voice of a trusted friend, a friend who makes you feel more hopeful and connected.

By making a purchase from Guideposts, you join our community in touching millions of lives, inspiring them to believe that all things are possible through faith, hope, and prayer. Your continued support allows us to provide uplifting resources to those in need. Whether through our online communities, websites, apps, or publications, we strive to inspire our audiences, bring them together, and comfort, uplift, entertain, and guide them.

To learn more, please go to guideposts.org.

Find more inspiring stories in these best-loved Guideposts fiction series!

Mysteries of Lancaster County
Follow the Classen sisters as they unravel clues and uncover hidden secrets in Mysteries of Lancaster County. As you get to know these women and their friends, you'll see how God brings each of them together for a fresh start in life.

Secrets of Wayfarers Inn
Retired schoolteachers find themselves owners of an old warehouse-turned-inn that is filled with hidden passages, buried secrets, and stunning surprises that will set them on a course to puzzling mysteries from the Underground Railroad.

Tearoom Mysteries Series
Mix one stately Victorian home, a charming lakeside town in Maine, and two adventurous cousins with a passion for tea and hospitality. Add a large scoop of intriguing mystery, and sprinkle generously with faith, family, and friends, and you have the recipe for *Tearoom Mysteries*.

Ordinary Women of the Bible
Richly imagined stories—based on facts from the Bible—have all the plot twists and suspense of a great mystery, while bringing you fascinating insights on what it was like to be a woman living in the ancient world.

To learn more about these books, visit Guideposts.org/Shop